USA by Numbers

A Statistical Portrait
of the United States

Library of Congress Cataloging-in-Publication Data

USA by numbers.

    Includes bibliographical references.
    1. United States–Population–Statistics. 2. Labor Supply–United States–Statistics. 3. Income distribution–United States–Statistics. 4. Man–Influence on nature–United States–Statistics. I. Zero Population Growth, Inc.

HA214.U8 1988   304.6'0973'021   88-58
ISBN 0-945219-00-8

Published by
Zero Population Growth, Inc.
1400 Sixteenth St., N.W.
Suite 320
Washington, D.C. 20036
202/332-2200

Printed in the United States of America by
Reproductions, Inc.
Rockville, MD

Design and typography by
Wordscape, Inc.
Washington, D.C.

Illustrations by
Caroline Mayer

First Edition, Second Printing

Acknowledgments

A book of this magnitude could not have been undertaken without the assistance and counsel of many individuals and organizations. First, I would like to extend my deepest appreciation to The Huber Foundation, The George Gund Foundation, and The Florence and John Schumann Foundation. Without their interest and financial support, quite simply, there would have been no book. I am also indebted to the members of our Board for their enthusiasm and guidance during this project.

The preliminary research that ultimately led to this publication was conducted by Jennifer Goldstein, a staff research associate. Once the project was given Board approval, we were lucky in ensnaring Annette Hatch-Clein who provided invaluable research assistance throughout this venture. I am also grateful to Mary Speare for her talents in wrinkling out vital statistics and demographic mysteries from sources 3,000 miles apart.

Nancy Debevoise coordinated endless piles of information and provided the narrative for this book. Special mention goes to Dianne Sherman and Elyse Chiland for their skillful production work. Drafts of the report were proofread by Deborah Brouse, Mark Esherick, Heather Francese, Nancy Jakubowski, Marjorie Macieira, Martha Morris, Rex Naylor and Jennifer Robbins.

To my staff and the many people who helped with information, contacts, and support, my sincerest thanks.

Susan Weber

Contents

Contents

Tables and Figures

Tables and Figures

Tables and Figures

Foreword

Although Americans are increasingly aware of population pressures in other parts of the world, many of us do not recognize the symptoms of overpopulation when we find them in our own backyards. We tend to believe that the United States has reached zero population growth, unaware that more than 2.3 million people are added to our population each year. Few of us recognize that traffic jams and overflowing garbage dumps, homelessness and child poverty, smog and water pollution are connected with – and consequences of – an expanding population.

But our lack of knowledge about our own population problems isn't due to a lack of curiosity. Public concern about the dramatic consequences of overpopulation is on the rise. News stories about the birth of the planet's five billionth inhabitant, escalating numbers of homeless American families, the "birth-dearth" controversy, our nation's burgeoning teen pregnancy problem, gridlock and violence on U.S. highways and the plight of desperate immigrants fleeing overpopulated and war-torn countries have all sparked Americans' interest in population issues.

Interest often generates action, and as public concern increases, so do the number of telephone and mail inquiries to organizations like Zero Population Growth. We're regularly deluged with requests for population statistics and trends analysis from reporters and researchers, elected officials and community activists, teachers and their students, opinion leaders and private citizens.

To meet the growing demand for comprehensive, easy-to-understand demographic data, we decided to develop an in-house reference notebook. The project quickly mushroomed into a year-long research project which culminated in the publication of *USA by Numbers*, our guided tour through the thicket of statistics that underlie and punctuate a host of American public policies, social problems and environmental issues. *USA by Numbers* tracks trends from A (acid rain) to Z (zero population growth predictions), from America's youngest mothers to her oldest citizens, from our fastest-growing cities to our shrinking water supply.

When we began to compile this unique statistical portrait of the United States, we wondered why no one else had undertaken such a project. As we quickly discovered, population-linked statistics are maddeningly difficult to ferret out from the maze of public and private institutions charged with tracking trends and recording data. And the population data that *is* available is presented in a manner which dampens enthusiasm rather than sparking interest. While mile-long computer printouts and thick books of charts may contain fascinating information and startling statistics about the effect of population growth on our quality of life, it is difficult to imagine materials any more intimidating.

Gathering and interpreting the data we found and putting it all between two covers took months of dedicated work. Now that we've got it, we want to share it.

Susan Weber
Executive Director
Zero Population Growth, Inc.
January 1988

Chapter 1

We The People:
Basic U.S. Demographics

We the People: Basic U.S. Demographics

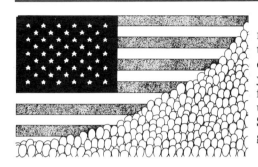

This chapter answers some of the most frequently asked questions about this country's population growth: "How quickly have we grown in the last 200 years?" "How big will we be 100 years from now?" "How far west has our population shifted?" "Hasn't the United States already reached zero population growth?"

Population Increases: 1790 to 1987

The U.S. population has grown from just under 4 million in 1790 to more than 240 million today (page 5). And we're still growing, by more than 2.3 million people each year. Our numbers grow by both natural increase (births minus deaths) and by immigration, which has increased steadily since the 1940s. Despite a decreasing growth *rate*, the *number* of people added to the population has remained large.

The Population Center Moves West

The center of the U.S. population has moved steadily westward since 1790 (page 6). The "population center" is the point at which the country would balance perfectly if it were a flat surface and every person on it had equal weight. Once east of Baltimore, Maryland, the population center now is located in Washington County, Missouri. (The **geographic** center of the country is west of Castle Rock, South Dakota.)

Shifts in the population center coincide with major historical trends such as the steady westward expansion of U.S. territories and the California gold rush. The population center marched almost due west until 1950, when it began to veer slightly southwestward. This shift has continued as job seekers, new immigrants and retired people migrate from economically depressed areas with harsh winters to booming Sunbelt states.

Population Projections

The U.S. population is projected to increase by nearly 70 million people during the next 100 years, reaching 310.8 million by 2080 (page 7). This is the equivalent of adding 115 cities the size of the city of Boston – or the combined populations of California, New Jersey, New York and Texas – to our population.

Three separate U.S. Census Bureau population projections, called the highest, middle and lowest series, differ in their assumptions about fertility, life expectancy and immigration levels. These projections point out the dramatic effect that seemingly small shifts in trends can have on the size of our population. For example, increasing our nation's current fertility rate by less than a half-percent while slightly increasing current legal immigration levels (now about 600,000 immigrants each year) would generate such rapid growth that our population would more than double in the next 100 years.

Attaining Zero Population Growth

The U.S. Census Bureau has projected U.S. population growth based on three different sets of assumptions about future average lifespan and fertility and immigration rates. One predicts that the U.S. could reach zero population growth (defined as the point at which a population stabilizes) as early as 2017 (page 8). This projection, however, is based on unrealistically low fertility rates and immigration levels.

A middle-range projection predicts that zpg may be reached by 2050, although this, too, is unlikely, since the social and economic upheavals generated by rapid population growth in developing nations are likely to force millions of people out of their countries, boosting U.S. immigration levels. At the high range, which considers the likelihood of increasing immigration rates and a small increase in fertility rates, demographers do not foresee that the U.S. will reach zpg.

Population Increases: 1790 to 1987

(Numbers in thousands)

Year	Population	Increase: Number	Increase: Percent
1790	3,929	–	–
1800	5,308	1,379	35.1
1810	7,240	1,932	36.4
1820	9,638	2,398	33.1
1830	12,861	3,223	33.4
1840	17,063	4,202	32.7
1850	23,192	6,129	35.9
1860	31,443	8,251	35.6
1870	38,558	7,115	22.6
1880	50,189	11,631	30.2
1890	62,980	12,791	25.5
1900	76,212	13,232	21.0
1910	92,228	16,016	21.0
1920	106,022	13,794	15.0
1930	123,203	17,181	16.2
1940	132,165	8,962	7.3
1950	151,326	19,161	14.5
1960	179,323	27,997	18.5
1970	203,302	23,979	13.4
1980	227,255	23,953	11.8
1981	229,637	2,382	1.1
1982	231,996	2,359	1.0
1983	234,284	2,288	1.0
1984	236,477	2,193	0.9
1985	238,741	2,264	1.0
1986	241,078	2,337	1.0
1987*	243,400	2,322	1.0

*Estimated figure

Note: Members of the armed forces and nationals overseas are not included.

Sources: For 1790 to 1970, U.S. Bureau of the Census, as cited in *The World Almanac and Book of Facts 1986*, (New York: Newspaper Enterprise Association, Inc.), 1985 and ZPG calculations; for 1980 to 1986, U.S. Bureau of the Census, "Estimates of the Population of the United States, by Age, Sex, and Race: 1980 to 1986," *Current Population Reports*, Series P-25, No. 1000, Table 2, 1987 and ZPG calculations; for 1987, U.S. Bureau of the Census, *U.S. Department of Commerce News*, CB87-205, December 30, 1987 and ZPG calculations.

The Population Center Moves West:
1790 to 1985

The **population center** is that point at which an imaginary, flat, weightless and rigid map of the United States would balance if every person on it had equal weight on the date of the census.

Year	Approximate Location
1790	23 miles east of Baltimore, MD
1850	23 miles southeast of Parkersburg, WV
1900	6 miles southeast of Columbus, IN
1950	8 miles north-northwest of Olney, IL in Richland County
1960	6.5 miles northwest of Centralia, IL in Clinton County
1970	5.3 miles east-southeast of the Mascoutah City Hall in St. Clair County, IL
1980	1/4 mile west of De Soto, MO in Jefferson County
1985	10 miles northwest of Potosi, MO in Washington County

Sources: For 1790 to 1980, U.S. Bureau of the Census, *Statistical Abstract of the United States: 1986*, Table 7; for 1985, U.S. Bureau of the Census, *U.S. Department of Commerce News*, April 28, 1986.

Population Projections

Year	Highest Series Projections	Middle Series Projections	Lowest Series Projections
1986		241,596,000*	
1990	254,122,000	249,657,000	245,753,000
1995	268,151,000	259,559,000	251,876,000
2000	281,542,000	267,955,000	256,098,000
2010	310,006,000	283,238,000	261,482,000
2030	369,775,000	304,807,000	257,443,000
2050	427,900,000	309,488,000	232,222,000
2080	531,178,000	310,762,000	191,118,000

*Actual figure for 1986. Total population includes armed forces and nationals overseas.

Notes: The highest series holds constant immigration at 750,000 per year, the fertility rate at 2.3, and the average lifespan at 77.4. The middle series maintains immigration at 450,000, the fertility rate at 1.9, and the average lifespan at 81.0. The lowest series maintains immigration at 250,000, a fertility rate of 1.6, and the average lifespan at 85.9. Currently, immigration stands at 571,000 per year (an average of 1981 to 1986 figures), the fertility rate is 1.8, and the average lifespan is 74.7.

Sources: For 1986, U.S. Bureau of the Census, "Estimates of the Population of the United States, by Age, Sex, and Race: 1980 to 1986," *Current Population Reports*, Series P-25, No. 1000, Table A, 1987; for 1990 to 2080, U.S. Bureau of the Census, "Projections of the Population of the United States, by Age, Sex, and Race: 1983 to 2080," *Current Population Reports*, Series P-25, No. 952, Table 2, Parts A, B, and C, 1984.

Attaining Zero Population Growth
(Numbers in thousands)

Zero population growth is achieved when a population stabilizes and its growth rate reaches zero. At this point, births plus immigration equal deaths plus emigration.

Series	Year	Population at ZPG	Population Increase from 1986	Percent Increase from 1986	Population in 2080	Population Change from 1986	Percent Change from 1986
Highest	ZPG not projected, population still growing				531,178	290,100	120.3%
Middle	2050	309,488	68,410	28.4%	310,762	69,684	28.9%
Lowest	2017	262,947	21,869	9.1%	191,118	−49,960	−20.7%

Sources: U.S. Bureau of the Census, "Projections of the Population of the United States, by Age, Sex, and Race: 1983 to 2080," *Current Population Reports,* Series P-25, No. 952, Table 2, Parts A, B, and C, 1984; ZPG calculations.

Chapter 2

States and Cities:
Population Size, Growth and Density

States and Cities: Population Size, Growth and Density

Changes in states' and cities' population size and density affect their economies, standard of living and environmental quality. Population shifts over time – from rural to urban areas, from the Rust Belt to the Sunbelt, from aging industrial cities to booming suburbs – have dramatically shaped life both in the places to which Americans are migrating and in those they've left behind.

Most and Least Populous States

America's most populous state has 56 times the residents of her least populous: more than 27 million people live in California, while fewer than 500,000 live in Wyoming (page 14).

States with the Highest and Lowest Growth

California, Texas and Florida led the nation in population gains from 1980 to 1987, adding a total of 8.8 million new residents (pages 15–17). Only three other states, Georgia, Arizona and Virginia, added more than 500,000 people. Four states lost residents: Iowa, Michigan, West Virginia and Ohio – all with depressed farm or industry-based economies.

Although California added more *people* from 1980 to 1987, Alaska's growth *rate*, 30.7%, was almost double that of California (pages 18–20). Nine of the top 10 growth states, by numbers and by rate, are in the South and West. The 10 states with the slowest growth rates, all located in the East and Midwest, either are losing residents or have relatively stable populations.

Regional Population Change

The West has tripled its population since 1940, from 14 million to 50 million, and the South has doubled its population, from 42 million to 84 million (page 21). The Northeast has added fewer residents to its population since 1940 than any other region of the country.

Ninety-one percent of the nation's population growth since 1980 has occurred in the South and West, where a total of more than 15 million residents have been added to the population. In contrast, the Northeast and Midwest, have added a total of 1.8 million residents to their populations since 1980.

Southern states have added nearly five times more people than the Northeast and Midwest combined since 1980. More people now live in the South than in any other region of the country.

Between 1940 and the present, the country as a whole experienced its highest growth rate, 18.5%, in the post-war, baby-boom decade between 1950 and 1960.

Although in terms of *numbers*, more than half of the nation's population growth has occurred in the South, the West has experienced the highest growth *rate*. The West's growth rate soared to 40.4% between 1940 and 1950 and continued to dramatically outpace other regions for the next two decades, until the South began to narrow the gap in 1980.

Differences in regional growth rates during the 1980s are dramatic. While the Midwest's population has grown by 1.1%, for example, the West's population has increased by 15%. On a smaller regional scale, western mountain states have experienced the nation's highest growth rate thus far this decade, 15.8%, while the Midwest's East North Central region has had the lowest, 0.5%.

States' Population Densities

The U.S. has an average of 69 people per square mile, though huge differences separate America's most and least densely populated states (page 23). New Jersey, for example, has more than 1,000 people per square mile, while Alaska has only one. Six of the 10 most densely populated states are in the Northeast. All of the least densely populated states are in the West and Midwest.

Six of the 10 most densely populated states are among the nation's 10 smallest in land area (page 24). Alaska, more than twice the size of Texas, ranks second to last in population size, behind Wyoming, and last in population density.

Life in the Big City

By 1986 the United States had eight cities with more than a million residents (page 26), although many metropolitan areas sprawl far into their suburbs and beyond, collecting millions of residents as the measured area expands. New York City, home to more than 7 million people, is in no danger of being passed by Los Angeles (3.3 million), Chicago (3 million) or Houston (1.7 million).

Since 1950, virtually all of the nation's fastest growing metropolitan areas have been southern and western cities, while almost all of the slowest growing are in the Northeast and Midwest (page 27). Metropolitan areas in Florida, California and Texas have recorded the largest growth rates each decade, while steel towns and other industrial cities in Pennsylvania, New York, New Jersey, Ohio and Illinois either have lost residents or have stable populations.

In 1800, the U.S. had only six cities with populations of up to 100,000 residents (page 29). The country didn't have a city with more than 100,000 people until 1820. Sixty years later, there were 20 cities with populations of 100,000 or more, and the population of New York City had reached the 1 million mark.

By 1980, the number of cities with fewer than 100,000 people had mushroomed to 2,730, while those with more than 100,000 inhabitants had jumped to 173. Six cities had reached populations of 1 million by then.

Movement from Rural to Urban Areas

The urbanization of America has been going on for almost 200 years (page 30). In 1790, only 5% of Americans lived in cities. A hundred years later, urban dwellers comprised 35% of the population, and by the 1910 census, the figure had risen to almost 46%. The most dramatic leap in rural to urban migration thus far this century took place between 1950 and 1970, when the percentage of urban dwellers rose from just under 59% to over 73%. The urban-to-rural ratio stabilized during the following decade in every region except the South Atlantic (Delaware, the District of Columbia, Maryland, Virginia and West Virginia), which showed nearly a 4% urban gain.

Regional differences were particularly striking in the first years of this century. While only 19% of those in the East South Central region (Kentucky, Tennessee, Alabama and Mississippi) were urban dwellers in 1910, fully 73% of New England residents lived in cities. The 1980 census showed that the population in the Pacific region (Alaska, California, Hawaii, Oregon and Washington) is the nation's most urbanized (87%), while the East South Central region is the least (56%).

Urbanization within states ranges from Vermont, where fewer than 34% of residents live in cities, to California, where more than 91% of the population is urban.

Most and Least Populous States: 1987

Most Populous States in 1987

Rank in 1987	State	Population (in thousands)	Rank in 1980
1	California	27,663	1
2	New York	17,825	2
3	Texas	16,789	3
4	Florida	12,023	7
5	Pennsylvania	11,936	4
6	Illinois	11,582	5
7	Ohio	10,784	6
8	Michigan	9,200	8
9	New Jersey	7,672	9
10	North Carolina	6,413	10
11	Georgia	6,222	13
12	Virginia	5,904	14
13	Massachusetts	5,855	11
14	Indiana	5,531	12
15	Missouri	5,103	15

Least Populous States in 1987

Rank in 1987	State	Population (in thousands)	Rank in 1980
1	Wyoming	490	2
2	Alaska	525	1
3	Vermont	548	3
4	Delaware	644	4
5	North Dakota	672	5
6	South Dakota	709	6
7	Montana	809	7
8	Rhode Island	986	11
9	Idaho	998	10
10	Nevada	1,007	8
11	New Hampshire	1,057	9
12	Hawaii	1,083	12
13	Maine	1,187	13
14	New Mexico	1,500	14
15	Nebraska	1,594	16

Source: U.S. Bureau of the Census, *U.S. Department of Commerce News,* CB-205, December 30, 1987.

States with Highest and Lowest Population Growth in Numbers: 1980 to 1987

States with the Highest Growth: 1980 to 1987

Rank in 1987	State	Change (in thousands)
1	California	3,995
2	Texas	2,559
3	Florida	2,277
4	Georgia	759
5	Arizona	668
6	Virginia	557
7	North Carolina	531
8*	Colorado	406
8*	Washington	406
10	Maryland	318
11	New Jersey	307
12	South Carolina	303
13	New York	267
14	Tennessee	264
15	Louisiana	255

States with the Lowest Growth: 1980 to 1987

Rank in 1987	State	Change (in thousands)
1	Iowa	-80
2	Michigan	-62
3	West Virginia	-52
4	Ohio	-14
5	South Dakota	18
6	North Dakota	19
7	Wyoming	21
8	Montana	23
9	Nebraska	25
10	Vermont	37
11	Rhode Island	39
12	Indiana	41
13	Delaware	50
14	Idaho	54
15	Maine	62

*Tie

Source: U.S. Bureau of the Census, *U.S. Department of Commerce News*, CB87-205, December 30, 1987.

States Ranked by Change in Numbers:
1980 to 1987

State	Population 1980 (in thousands)	Estimated Population 1987 (in thousands)	Growth in Numbers (in thousands)	Rank by Growth in Numbers
California	23,668	27,663	3,995	1
Texas	14,229	16,789	2,559	2
Florida	9,746	12,023	2,277	3
Georgia	5,463	6,222	759	4
Arizona	2,718	3,386	668	5
Virginia	5,347	5,904	557	6
North Carolina	5,882	6,413	531	7
Colorado	2,890	3,296	406	8*
Washington	4,132	4,538	406	8*
Maryland	4,217	4,535	318	10
New Jersey	7,365	7,672	307	11
South Carolina	3,122	3,425	303	12
New York	17,558	17,825	267	13
Tennessee	4,591	4,855	264	14
Louisiana	4,206	4,461	255	15
Oklahoma	3,025	3,272	247	16
Utah	1,461	1,680	219	17
Nevada	800	1,007	207	18
New Mexico	1,303	1,500	197	19
Alabama	3,894	4,083	189	20
Missouri	4,917	5,103	186	21
Minnesota	4,076	4,246	170	22
Illinois	11,427	11,582	156	23
New Hampshire	921	1,057	136	24
Alaska	402	525	123	25
Hawaii	965	1,083	118	26*
Massachusetts	5,737	5,855	118	26*
Kansas	2,364	2,476	112	28

Continued, next page

States Ranked by Change in Numbers: 1980 to 1987 (Cont.)

State	Population 1980 (in thousands)	Estimated Population 1987 (in thousands)	Growth in Numbers (in thousands)	Rank by Growth in Numbers
Connecticut	3,108	3,211	104	29*
Mississippi	2,521	2,625	104	29*
Arkansas	2,286	2,388	102	31
Wisconsin	4,706	4,807	101	32
Oregon	2,633	2,724	91	33
Pennsylvania	11,864	11,936	72	34
Kentucky	3,661	3,727	66	35
Maine	1,125	1,187	62	36
Idaho	944	998	54	37
Delaware	594	644	50	38
Indiana	5,490	5,531	41	39
Rhode Island	947	986	39	40
Vermont	511	548	37	41
Nebraska	1,570	1,594	25	42
Montana	787	809	23	43
Wyoming	470	490	21	44
North Dakota	653	672	19	45
South Dakota	691	709	18	46
Ohio	10,798	10,784	−14	47
West Virginia	1,950	1,897	−52	48
Michigan	9,262	9,200	−62	49
Iowa	2,914	2,834	−80	50

*Tie

Source: U.S. Bureau of the Census, *U.S. Department of Commerce News*, CB87-205, December 30, 1987.

States with the Fastest and Slowest Population Growth Rates: 1980 to 1987

States with the Fastest Growth Rates: 1980 to 1987

Rank in 1987	State	Growth Rate
1	Alaska	30.7%
2	Nevada	25.8
3	Arizona	24.6
4	Florida	23.4
5	Texas	18.0
6	California	16.9
7	New Mexico	15.1
8	Utah	15.0
9	New Hampshire	14.8
10	Colorado	14.1
11	Georgia	13.9
12	Hawaii	12.2
13	Virginia	10.4
14	Washington	9.8
15	South Carolina	9.7

States with the Slowest Growth Rates: 1980 to 1987

Rank in 1987	State	Growth Rate
1*	Iowa	−2.7%
1*	West Virginia	−2.7
3	Michigan	−0.7
4	Ohio	−0.1
5	Pennsylvania	0.6
6	Indiana	0.7
7	Illinois	1.4
8	New York	1.5
9	Nebraska	1.6
10	Kentucky	1.8
11*	Massachusetts	2.1
11*	Wisconsin	2.1
13	South Dakota	2.7
14*	North Dakota	2.9
14*	Montana	2.9

*Tie

Source: U.S. Bureau of the Census, *U.S. Department of Commerce News*, CB87-205, December 30, 1987.

States Ranked by Growth Rates: 1980 to 1987

State	Population 1980 (in thousands)	Estimated Population 1987 (in thousands)	Percent Change	Rank by Growth Rate
Alaska	402	525	30.7	1
Nevada	800	1,007	25.8	2
Arizona	2,718	3,386	24.6	3
Florida	9,746	12,023	23.4	4
Texas	14,229	16,789	18.0	5
California	23,668	27,663	16.9	6
New Mexico	1,303	1,500	15.1	7
Utah	1,461	1,680	15.0	8
New Hampshire	921	1,057	14.8	9
Colorado	2,890	3,296	14.1	10
Georgia	5,463	6,222	13.9	11
Hawaii	965	1,083	12.2	12
Virginia	5,347	5,904	10.4	13
Washington	4,132	4,538	9.8	14
South Carolina	3,122	3,425	9.7	15
North Carolina	5,882	6,413	9.0	16
Delaware	594	644	8.3	17
Oklahoma	3,025	3,272	8.2	18
Maryland	4,217	4,535	7.5	19
Vermont	511	548	7.2	20
Louisiana	4,206	4,461	6.1	21
Idaho	944	998	5.8	22
Tennessee	4,591	4,855	5.7	23
Maine	1,125	1,187	5.5	24
Alabama	3,894	4,083	4.9	25
Kansas	2,364	2,476	4.7	26
Arkansas	2,286	2,388	4.5	27

Continued, next page

States Ranked by Growth Rates: 1980 to 1987 (Cont.)

State	Population 1980 (in thousands)	Estimated Population 1987 (in thousands)	Percent Change	Rank by Growth Rate
Wyoming	470	490	4.4	28
Minnesota	4,076	4,246	4.2	29*
New Jersey	7,365	7,672	4.2	29*
Mississippi	2,521	2,625	4.1	31*
Rhode Island	947	986	4.1	31*
Missouri	4,917	5,103	3.8	33
Oregon	2,633	2,724	3.4	34
Connecticut	3,108	3,211	3.3	35
Montana	787	809	2.9	36*
North Dakota	653	672	2.9	36*
South Dakota	691	709	2.7	38
Wisconsin	4,706	4,807	2.1	39*
Massachusetts	5,737	5,855	2.1	39*
Kentucky	3,661	3,727	1.8	41
Nebraska	1,570	1,594	1.6	42
New York	17,558	17,825	1.5	43
Illinois	11,427	11,582	1.4	44
Indiana	5,490	5,531	0.7	45
Pennsylvania	11,864	11,936	0.6	46
Ohio	10,798	10,784	−0.1	47
Michigan	9,262	9,200	−0.7	48
West Virginia	1,950	1,897	−2.7	49*
Iowa	2,914	2,834	−2.7	49*

*Tie.

Source: U.S. Bureau of the Census, *U.S. Department of Commerce News*, CB87-205, December 30, 1987.

Population Change by Region: 1940 to 1987

(Numbers in thousands)

Region	Population 1940	Population 1950	Percent Change 1940 to 1950	Population 1960	Percent Change 1950 to 1960
UNITED STATES	132,165	151,326	14.5	179,323	18.5
NORTHEAST	35,977	39,478	9.7	44,678	13.2
New England	8,437	9,314	10.4	10,509	12.8
Middle Atlantic	27,539	30,164	9.5	34,168	13.3
MIDWEST	40,143	44,461	10.8	51,619	16.1
East North Central	26,626	30,399	14.2	36,225	19.2
West North Central	13,517	14,061	4.0	15,394	9.5
SOUTH	41,666	47,197	13.3	54,973	16.5
South Atlantic	17,823	21,182	18.8	25,972	22.6
East South Central	10,778	11,477	6.5	12,050	5.0
West South Central	13,065	14,538	11.3	16,951	16.6
WEST	14,379	20,190	40.4	28,053	38.9
Mountain	4,150	5,075	22.3	6,855	35.1
Pacific	10,229	15,115	47.8	21,198	40.2

Continued, next page

Population Change by Region: 1940 to 1987 (Cont.)
(Numbers in thousands)

Region	Population 1970	Percent Change 1960 to 1970	Population 1980	Percent Change 1970 to 1980	Population 1987	Percent Change 1980 to 1987
UNITED STATES	203,302	13.4	226,546	11.4	243,000	7.4
NORTHEAST	49,016	9.8	49,137	0.2	50,278	2.3
New England	11,848	12.7	12,349	4.2	12,844	4.0
Middle Atlantic	37,213	8.9	36.788	-1.1	37,433	1.8
MIDWEST	56,589	9.6	58,867	4.0	59,538	1.1
East North Central	40,262	11.1	41,682	3.5	41,904	0.5
West North Central	16,327	6.1	17.184	5.2	17,634	2.6
SOUTH	62,812	14.3	75,369	20.0	83,884	11.3
South Atlantic	30,678	18.1	36,960	20.5	41,684	12.8
East South Central	12,808	6.3	14,666	14.5	15,290	4.3
West South Central	19,326	14.0	23,743	22.9	26,910	13.3
WEST	34,838	24.2	43,171	23.9	49,700	15.1
Mountain	8,289	20.9	11,372	37.2	13,167	15.8
Pacific	26,549	25.2	31,800	19.8	36,533	14.9

Notes: New England includes ME, NH, VT, MA, RI and CT; Middle Atlantic includes NY, NJ and PA; East North Central includes OH, IN, IL, MI and WI; West North Central includes MN, IA, MO, ND, SD, NE and KS; South Atlantic includes DE, MD, DC, VA, WV, NC, SC, GA and FL; East South Central includes KY, TN, AL and MS; West South Central includes AR, LA, OK and TX; Mountain includes MT, ID, WY, CO, NM, AZ, UT and NV; Pacific includes WA, OR, CA, AK and HI.

Source: For 1940 to 1980, U.S. Bureau of the Census, *Statistical Abstract of the United States: 1986*, Table 11, 1985; for 1986, U.S. Bureau of the Census, *U.S. Department of Commerce News*, CB87-205, December 30, 1987.

Most and Least Densely Populated States: 1987

Most Densely Populated States: 1987

Rank	State	People per Square Mile
1	New Jersey	1,027
2	Rhode Island	935
3	Massachusetts	748
4	Connecticut	659
5	Maryland	461
6	New York	376
7	Delaware	333
8	Pennsylvania	266
9	Ohio	263
10	Florida	222

Least Densely Populated States: 1987

Rank	State	People per Square Mile
1	Alaska	1
2	Wyoming	5
3	Montana	6
4*	Nevada	9
4*	South Dakota	9
6	North Dakota	10
7*	Idaho	12
7*	New Mexico	12
9	Utah	20
10	Nebraska	21

*Tie

Sources: U.S. Bureau of the Census, *U.S. Department of Commerce News*, CB87-205, December 30, 1987; U.S. Bureau of the Census, *State and Metropolitan Area Data Book 1982*, Table C, 1982.

States Ranked by Density: 1987

State	Rank by 1987 Density	People per Square Mile	Rank by 1987 Population	Estimated 1987 Population (in thousands)	Rank by Land Area	Land Area in Square Miles
New Jersey	1	1,027	9	7,672	46	7,468
Rhode Island	2	935	43	986	50	1,055
Massachusetts	3	748	13	5,855	45	7,824
Connecticut	4	659	28	3,211	48	4,872
Maryland	5	461	19	4,535	42	9,837
New York	6	376	2	17,825	30	47,377
Delaware	7	333	47	644	49	1,932
Pennsylvania	8	266	5	11,936	32	44,888
Ohio	9	263	7	10,784	35	41,004
Florida	10	222	4	12,023	26	54,153
Illinois	11	208	6	11,582	24	55,645
California	12	177	1	27,663	3	156,299
Hawaii	13	169	39	1,083	47	6,425
Michigan	14	162	8	9,200	22	56,954
Indiana	15	154	14	5,531	38	35,932
Virginia	16	149	12	5,904	36	39,704
North Carolina	17	131	10	6,413	29	48,843
Tennessee	18*	118	16	4,855	34	41,155
New Hampshire	18*	118	40	1,057	44	8,993
South Carolina	20	113	24	3,425	40	30,203
Georgia	21	107	11	6,222	21	58,056
Louisiana	22	100	20	4,461	33	44,521
Kentucky	23	94	23	3,727	37	39,669
Wisconsin	24	88	17	4,807	25	54,426
Alabama	25	80	22	4,083	28	50,767
West Virginia	26	79	34	1,897	41	24,119
Missouri	27	74	15	5,103	18	68,945
Washington	28	68	18	4,538	20	66,511
Texas	29	64	3	16,789	2	262,017
Vermont	30	59	48	548	43	9,273

Continued, next page

States Ranked by Density: 1987 (Cont.)

State	Rank by 1987 Density	People per Square Mile	Rank by 1987 Population	Estimated 1987 Population (in thousands)	Rank by Land Area	Land Area in Square Miles
Mississippi	31	56	31	2,625	31	47,233
Minnesota	32	53	21	4,246	14	79,548
Iowa	33	51	29	2,834	23	55,965
Oklahoma	34	48	27	3,272	19	68,655
Arkansas	35	46	33	2,388	27	52,078
Maine	36	38	38	1,187	39	30,995
Colorado	37	32	26	3,296	8	103,595
Kansas	38*	30	32	2,476	13	81,778
Arizona	38*	30	25	3,386	6	113,508
Oregon	40	28	30	2,724	10	96,184
Nebraska	41	21	36	1,594	15	76,644
Utah	42	20	35	1,680	12	82,073
New Mexico	43*	12	37	1,500	5	121,335
Idaho	43*	12	42	998	11	82,412
North Dakota	45	10	46	672	17	69,300
South Dakota	46*	9	45	709	16	75,952
Nevada	46*	9	41	1,007	7	109,894
Montana	48	6	44	809	4	145,388
Wyoming	49	5	50	490	9	96,989
Alaska	50	1	49	525	1	570,833

*Tie.

Sources: U.S. Bureau of the Census, *U.S. Department of Commerce News*, CB87-205, December 30, 1987; and U.S. Bureau of the Census, *State and Metropolitan Data Book 1982*, Table C., 1982.

Largest Cities: 1986

City and State	Population 1986	Rank in 1986	Population 1980	Rank in 1980	Percent Change, 1980 to 1986	Rank by Change
New York, NY	7,262,700	1	7,071,639	1	2.7	12
Los Angeles, CA	3,259,300	2	2,968,528	3	9.8	9
Chicago, IL	3,009,530	3	3,005,072	2	0.1	17
Houston, TX	1,728,910	4	1,611,382	5	7.3	10
Philadelphia, PA	1,642,900	5	1,688,210	4	−2.7	21
Detroit, MI	1,086,220	6	1,203,369	6	−9.7	25
San Diego, CA	1,015,190	7	875,538	8	16.0	1
Dallas, TX	1,003,520	8	904,599	7	10.9	7
San Antonio, TX	914,350	9	810,353	9	12.8	5
Phoenix, AZ	894,070	10	790,183	10	13.1	3
Baltimore, MD	752,800	11	786,741	11	−4.3	22
San Francisco, CA	749,000	12	678,974	13	10.3	8
Indianapolis, IN	719,820	13	700,807	12	2.7	11
San Jose, CA	712,080	14	629,402	17	13.1	4
Memphis, TN	652,640	15	646,170	14	1.0	15
Washington, DC	626,000	16	638,432	15	−1.9	20
Jacksonville, FL	610,030	17	540,920	22	12.8	6
Milwaukee, WI	605,090	18	636,298	16	−4.9	23
Boston, MA	573,600	19	562,994	20	1.9	14
Columbus, OH	566,030	20	565,032	19	8.2	16
New Orleans, LA	554,500	21	557,927	21	−0.6	18
Cleveland, OH	535,830	22	573,822	18	−6.6	24
Denver, CO	505,000	23	492,694	24	2.5	13
El Paso, TX	491,800	24	425,259	28	15.6	2
Seattle, WA	486,200	25	493,846	23	−1.5	19

Source: U.S. Bureau of the Census, *U.S. Department of Commerce News,* CB87-165, October 16, 1987

Fastest and Slowest Growing Metropolitan Areas by Decade: 1950 to 1984

(Population over 250,000)

		Fastest Growing				Slowest Growing	
Years	Rank	Metro Area	Percent Change	Rank	Metro Area	Percent Change
1950-1960:						
	1	Fort Lauderdale-Hollywood, FL	298	1	Wilkes Barre-Hazleton, PA	−12
	2	Orlando, FL	125	2	Jersey City, NJ	−6
	3	San Jose, CA	121	3	Johnstown, PA	−4
	4	Phoenix, AZ	100	4*	Huntington-Ashland, WV-KY-OH	4
	5*	Miami, FL	89	4*	New Bedford-Fall River, MA-RI	4
	5*	Tampa-St. Petersburg, FL	89	6	Providence-Pawtucket Warwick, MA-RI	5
	7	Tucson, AZ	88	7	Charlestown, WV	6
	8	San Diego, CA	86	8	Worcester, MA	7
	9	Sacramento, CA	81	9	Reading, PA	8
	10	Albuquerque, NM	80	10	Pittsburgh, PA	9
1960-1970:						
	1	Las Vegas, NV	115	1	Johnstown, PA	−6
	2	Anaheim-Santa Ana-Garden Grove, CA	102	2	Duluth-Superior, MN-WI	−4
	3	Oxnard-Ventura, CA	90	3*	Wilkes-Barre-Hazleton, PA	−1
	4	Fort Lauderdale-Hollywood, FL	86	3*	Jersey City, NJ	−1
	5	San Jose, CA	66	5*	Huntington-Ashland, WV-KY-OH	0
	6	Santa Barbara, CA	56	5*	Pittsburgh, PA	0
	7	West Palm Beach, FL	53	7	Wichita, KS	2
	8	Phoenix, AZ	46	8*	Birmingham, AL	3
	9	San Bernardino-Riverside-Ontario, CA	41	8*	Utica-Rome, NY	3
	10	Houston, TX	40	8*	South Bend, IN	3

Continued, next page

Fastest and Slowest Growing
Metropolitan Areas by Decade: 1950 to 1984 (Cont.)

		Fastest Growing				Slowest Growing	
Years	Rank	Metro Area	Percent Change	Rank	Metro Area	Percent Change
1970 -1980:							
	1	Las Vegas, NV	70	1*	Jersey City, NJ	– 8
	2	West Palm Beach, FL	65	1*	Buffalo, NY	– 8
	3	Fort Lauderdale-Hollywood, FL	64	1*	Cleveland, OH	– 8
	4	McAllen-Pharr-Edinburg, TX	56	4	New York, NY	– 7
	5*	Phoenix, AZ	55	5*	Utica-Rome, NY	– 6
	5*	Orlando, FL	55	5*	Pittsburgh, PA	– 6
	7	Daytona Beach, FL	53	7*	Paterson-Clifton-Passaic, NJ	– 5
	8	Tucson, AZ	51	7*	Newark, NJ	– 5
	9	Austin, TX	49	9*	Akron, OH	– 3
	10	Santa Rosa, CA	46	9*	Dayton, OH	– 3
1980 -1984:							
	1	Fort Myers-Cape Coral, FL	23	1	Duluth-Superior, MN-WI	– 5
	2	Melbourne-Titusville-Palm Bay, FL	21	2*	Detroit, MI	– 4
	3*	Austin, TX	20	2*	Flint, MI	– 4
	3*	West Palm Beach, FL	20	4*	Eugene-Springfield, OR	– 3
	5	McAllen-Pharr-Edinburg, TX	19	4*	Buffalo, NY	– 3
	6	Orlando, FL	18	4*	Peoria, IL	– 3
	7*	San Bernardino-Riverside-Ontario, CA	16	4*	Youngstown-Warren, OH	– 3
	7*	Daytona Beach, FL	16	8*	Pittsburgh, PA	– 2
	7*	Las Vegas, NV	16	8*	Johnstown, PA	– 2
	10	Houston, TX	15	8*	Gary-Hammond-East Chicago, IN	– 2

*Tie.

**The percentage growth for 1970–1980 is not adjusted for changes in census enumeration.

Sources: Alden Speare and William Frye, *Regional and Metropolitan Growth and Decline in the United States,* (Russell Sage, Inc.), forthcoming publication of the U.S. Bureau of the Census; U.S. Bureau of the Census, "Patterns of Metropolitan Area and County Population Growth: 1980 to 1984," *Current Population Reports,* Series P-25, No. 976, Table 5, 1985.

Number of Cities by
Population Size: 1800 to 1980

City Size	Number of Cities				
	1800	**1820**	**1840**	**1860**	**1880**
1,000,000 or more	0	0	0	0	1
500,000 to 999,000	0	0	0	2	3
250,000 to 499,000	0	0	1	1	4
100,000 to 249,000	0	1	2	6	12
100,000 or more	0	1	3	9	20
50,000 to 99,999	1	2	2	7	15
25,000 to 49,000	2	2	7	19	42
10,000 to 24,999	3	8	25	58	146
10,000 to 99,999	6	12	34	84	203

City Size	Number of Cities				
	1900	**1920**	**1940**	**1960**	**1980**
1,000,000 or more	3	3	5	5	6
500,000 to 999,000	3	9	9	16	16
250,000 to 499,000	9	13	23	30	34
100,000 to 249,000	23	43	55	81	117
100,000 or more	38	68	92	132	173
50,000 to 99,999	40	76	107	201	290
25,000 to 49,000	82	143	213	432	675
10,000 to 24,999	280	465	665	1,134	1,765
10,000 to 99,999	402	684	985	1,767	2,730

Sources: U.S. Bureau of the Census, *Historical Statistics of the United States, Colonial Times to 1970,* Part 1, Series A-43-56, 1975; U.S. Bureau of the Census, *Statistical Abstract of the United States: 1986,* Table 17, 1985.

Urban Percentage of the Population by Division and State: 1790 to 1980

Division and State	1790	1810	1830	1850	1870	1890	1910	1930	1950	1970	1980
UNITED STATES	5.1	7.3	8.8	15.3	25.7	35.1	45.7	56.2	58.8	73.5	73.7
NEW ENGLAND	7.5	10.1	14.0	28.7	44.4	61.6	73.3	77.3	74.8	76.3	75.1
Maine	0.0	3.1	3.3	13.6	21.1	28.1	35.3	40.4	41.0	50.7	47.5
New Hampshire	3.5	3.3	4.8	17.0	26.1	39.3	51.7	58.7	58.5	56.4	52.1
Vermont	0.0	0.0	0.0	1.9	6.9	15.4	27.8	33.1	36.5	32.2	33.9
Massachusetts	13.5	21.4	31.1	50.7	66.7	82.0	89.0	90.1	86.7	84.5	83.8
Rhode Island	18.8	23.4	30.9	55.4	74.7	85.3	91.0	92.4	87.0	86.8	87.0
Connecticut	2.9	6.1	9.4	15.9	33.0	50.9	65.7	70.4	69.3	77.3	78.8
MIDDLE ATLANTIC	8.7	11.5	14.2	25.5	44.2	58.0	71.2	77.7	75.6	81.7	80.6
New York	11.5	12.6	15.0	28.2	49.9	65.1	78.9	83.6	80.3	85.5	84.6
New Jersey	0.0	2.4	5.6	17.6	43.7	62.6	76.4	82.6	81.0	88.9	89.0
Pennsylvania	10.1	12.8	15.3	23.6	37.3	48.6	60.4	67.8	66.5	71.4	69.3
EAST NORTH CENTRAL		1.1	2.5	9.0	21.6	37.9	52.7	66.4	66.3	74.7	73.3
Ohio		1.3	3.9	12.2	25.6	41.1	55.9	67.8	67.3	75.3	73.3
Indiana		0.0	0.0	4.6	14.8	26.9	42.4	55.4	56.4	64.9	64.2
Illinois		0.0	0.0	7.5	23.5	44.9	61.7	73.9	74.5	83.1	83.3
Michigan		0.0	0.0	7.3	20.1	34.9	47.2	68.2	65.4	73.8	70.7
Wisconsin				9.5	19.6	33.2	43.0	52.9	56.7	65.9	64.2
WEST NORTH CENTRAL		0.0	3.6	10.3	19.0	25.8	33.2	41.8	49.9	63.6	63.9
Minnesota				0.0	16.1	33.8	40.9	49.1	53.9	66.4	66.9
Iowa				5.2	13.1	21.2	30.6	39.6	46.9	57.2	58.6
Missouri		0.0	3.6	11.9	25.0	32.0	42.3	51.2	57.9	70.1	68.1
North Dakota					0.0	5.8	10.9	16.6	26.6	44.2	48.7
South Dakota					0.0	8.3	13.0	18.9	33.1	44.6	46.5
Nebraska					17.9	27.5	26.1	35.3	45.8	61.5	62.9
Kansas					14.3	18.9	29.1	38.8	47.4	66.0	66.7

Continued, next page

Urban Percentage of the Population by Division and State: 1790 to 1980 (Cont.)

Division and State	1790	1810	1830	1850	1870	1890	1910	1930	1950	1970	1980
SOUTH ATLANTIC	2.3	4.6	6.2	9.8	14.4	19.5	25.4	36.1	43.8	63.6	67.1
Delaware	0.0	0.0	0.0	15.2	24.8	42.3	48.0	51.7	46.5	72.3	70.7
Maryland	4.4	12.3	20.4	32.2	37.8	47.6	50.8	59.7	60.9	76.6	80.3
District of Columbia		86.7	90.0	92.3	91.7	100.0	100.0	100.0	100.0	100.0	100.0
Virginia	1.7	3.6	4.8	8.0	11.9	17.1	23.1	32.5	41.4	63.1	66.0
West Virginia	0.0	0.0	0.0	3.6	8.1	10.6	18.7	28.5	32.0	38.9	36.2
North Carolina	0.0	0.0	1.4	2.4	3.4	7.2	14.4	25.6	30.5	44.9	48.0
South Carolina	6.4	6.0	5.9	7.3	8.6	10.1	14.9	21.3	30.8	47.5	54.1
Georgia	0.0	2.0	2.7	4.3	8.4	14.0	20.7	30.8	41.4	60.3	62.4
Florida			0.0	0.0	8.0	19.7	29.1	51.8	56.5	80.5	84.3
EAST SOUTH CENTRAL	0.0	0.6	1.5	4.2	8.8	12.7	18.7	28.1	35.5	54.6	55.7
Kentucky	0.0	1.0	2.3	7.5	14.8	19.2	24.2	30.6	33.5	52.3	50.9
Tennessee	0.0	0.0	0.9	2.2	7.5	13.5	20.2	34.3	38.4	58.7	60.4
Alabama		0.0	1.0	4.5	6.3	10.0	17.3	28.1	40.1	58.4	60.0
Mississippi		0.0	2.2	1.8	4.0	5.4	11.5	16.9	27.6	44.5	47.3
WEST SOUTH CENTRAL		21.8	18.7	15.1	13.3	15.1	22.3	36.4	52.7	72.6	73.4
Arkansas		0.0	0.0	0.0	2.5	6.5	12.9	20.7	32.3	50.0	51.6
Louisiana		22.1	21.3	25.9	27.9	25.4	30.0	39.7	51.4	66.0	68.6
Oklahoma						3.5	19.3	34.3	47.4	68.0	67.3
Texas				3.8	6.7	15.7	24.1	41.0	59.8	79.7	79.6

Continued, next page

Urban Percentage of the Population by Division and State: 1790 to 1980 (Cont.)

Division and State	1790	1810	1830	1850	1870	1890	1910	1930	1950	1970	1980
MOUNTAIN				6.8	12.3	29.2	35.9	39.4	49.2	73.0	76.4
Montana					14.3	27.3	35.4	33.6	42.8	53.5	52.9
Idaho					0.0	0.0	21.5	29.2	39.7	54.0	54.0
Wyoming					0.0	33.3	29.5	31.0	49.8	60.5	62.8
Colorado					12.5	45.0	50.3	50.2	57.4	78.4	80.6
New Mexico				8.1	5.4	6.3	14.4	25.3	46.3	69.7	72.1
Arizona					30.0	9.1	30.9	34.4	36.5	79.4	83.8
Utah				0.0	18.4	35.5	46.4	52.4	62.8	80.4	84.4
Nevada					16.7	34.0	15.9	37.4	52.5	80.8	85.4
PACIFIC				6.6	32.0	41.9	55.0	66.6	63.5	85.9	86.6
Washington				0.0	0.0	35.6	53.1	56.6	53.6	72.5	73.5
Oregon				0.0	8.8	27.7	45.6	51.4	48.1	67.1	67.9
California				7.5	37.1	48.6	61.7	73.3	68.1	90.8	91.3
Alaska						0.0	9.4	13.6	26.4	48.2	64.4
Hawaii							30.7	53.8	69.0	83.0	86.5

Notes: Blanks mean no census taken for a state at that date. 0.0% indicates only rural population. Urban areas include cities and the densely-settled fringe areas surrounding the central cities. Urban areas also include urban "places," those towns and/or cities with a population of 2,500 or more. For a more complete definition of urban areas, refer to the U.S. Bureau of the Census.

Sources: For 1790 to 1960, U.S. Bureau of the Census, *Historical Statistics of the United States, From Colonial Times to 1970,* Part 1, Chapter A, 1975; for 1970 and 1980, U.S. Bureau of the Census, *State and Metropolitan Area Data Book 1982,* Table C, 1982.

Chapter 3

The Melting Pot:
Legal and Illegal Immigration

The Melting Pot:
Legal and Illegal Immigration

Population pressures in developing nations help generate political instability, social upheaval, war, famine and mass migrations of families seeking better lives in other countries. More than a million people enter the United States each year as both legal and illegal immigrants.

Legal Immigration

More than 53 million immigrants have been legally admitted to the United States since 1820 (page 37). The greatest wave of immigration took place between 1901 and 1910, when almost 9 million people, the vast majority from Europe, arrived in the United States. Legal immigration has increased steadily since the 1940s, and we are now adding about 600,000 new legal residents to our population each year.

Origin of Legal Immigrants

Legal immigrants' countries of origin have changed markedly since the turn of the century, when virtually all newcomers came from Europe (page 38). From 1901 through 1960, for example, Germany contributed more immigrants than all of Asia combined. However, during the next 20 years, Asia passed Europe as the continent of origin for the largest numbers, and during the 1980s, three times more Asian immigrants than Europeans entered the United States.

Today, the vast majority of immigrants come from countries in South and Central America and Asia (page 39). Mexico was the leading contributor nation of legal immigrants in 1985, followed by four Asian nations: the Philippines, Korea, China and India.

The federal government did not collect data on the destinations of new immigrants during fiscal years 1980 and 1981, but there is information for the four previous and five subsequent years (page 40). Two states, California and New York, were named as intended destinations by 44% of all new immigrants who arrived in this country between 1982 and 1986.

Although many of the 15 states most favored by new immigrants have risen and dropped slightly in the ranks during the past decade, Washington state has dramatically increased its appeal. Named by fewer than 30,000 newcomers from 1976 through 1979, Washington was favored by more than 53,000 immigrants from 1982 through 1986.

Immigration's Effect on Population Growth

Because of a reduction in U.S. fertility rates since the 1970s, immigration is having a greater and greater impact on U.S. population growth (page 41). New immigrants contributed almost 30% of our nation's net population increase between 1980 and 1985. Not since the first decade of this century, when our population was much smaller and immigration levels were at their highest ever, has immigration comprised a greater proportion of our population growth. In the future, immigration promises to play an even more prominent role in population growth as birth rates remain stable and the number of immigrants continues to rise.

Illegal Immigration

Many who cannot enter the United States legally do so illegally, risking apprehension, jail and deportation. No one knows how many illegal immigrants enter this country undetected each year; estimates varied from 500,000 to 1.5 million prior to the implementation of immigration-reform legislation passed in 1986.

The number of illegal aliens apprehended has risen dramatically, from 910,000 in 1980 to 1,200,000 in 1987 (page 42). The U.S. Immigration and Naturalization Service notes that many people who attempt to enter the country illegally are apprehended and returned to their countries, only to be caught again several days or months later. The agency estimates that for every illegal alien apprehended, two to three others cross the border undetected.

Legal Immigration: 1820 to 1986

Years	Immigrants Admitted
Total	**53,122,066**
1820	8,385
1821-30	143,438
1831-40	599,125
1841-50	1,713,251
1851-60	2,598,214
1861-70	2,314,824
1871-80	2,812,191
1881-90	5,246,613
1891-00	3,687,564
1901-10	8,795,386
1911-20	5,735,811
1921-30	4,107,209
1931-40	528,431
1941-50	1,035,039
1951-60	2,515,479
1961-70	3,321,677
1971-80	4,493,314
1980	530,639
1981	596,600
1982	594,131
1983	559,763
1984	543,903
1985	570,009
1986	601,708

Sources: For 1820 to 1985, Immigration and Naturalization Service, *1985 Statistical Yearbook of the Immigration and Naturalization Service,* Table IMM 1.1., 1986; for 1986, the Immigration and Naturalization Service, 1987.

Origin of Legal Immigrants and Largest Contributors: 1901 to 1985

(Numbers in thousands)

Contributor*	Total† 1901-1985	1901- 1920	1921- 1940	1941- 1960	1961- 1980	1981- 1985
All Countries	**33,397**	**14,531**	**4,636**	**3,551**	**7,815**	**2,864**
Europe	**19,394**	**12,378**	**2,811**	**1,947**	**1,924**	**334**
Italy	4,290	3,155	523	243	343	24
Germany††	2,021	485	526	704	265	40
United Kingdom†††	2,012	867	372	344	352	76
Asia	**4,259**	**571**	**128**	**186**	**2,016**	**1,358**
Philippines**	703	–	–	19	453	231
Korea**	473	–	–	6	302	165
China***	430	42	35	26	159	167
America	**9,311**	**1,506**	**1,677**	**1,352**	**3,699**	**1,078**
Canada****	3,153	921	1,033	550	583	65
Mexico	2,540	269	482	360	1,094	336
Cuba**	603	–	–	79	473	51
Africa	**228**	**16**	**8**	**21**	**110**	**73**
Australia & New Zealand	**114**	**24**	**11**	**25**	**43**	**11**
Pacific Isles (U.S. Adm.)	**14**	**2**	**1**	**7**	**4**	**.7**
Not Specified	**77**	**35**	**.2**	**13**	**20**	**9**

*Data for the years 1980 to 1983 refer to country of birth for all countries listed. All other years refer to country of last permanent residence.
**First year figures were recorded in 1951. Beginning with the year 1951, Asia includes the Philippines.
***Beginning with the year 1957, China includes Taiwan.
****Includes Newfoundland.
†Numbers do not add up to total due to rounding.
††From 1938-1945, Austria is included in Germany.
†††From 1925 to present, data for United Kingdom refer to England, Scotland, Wales and Northern Ireland. Prior to 1925, data for Northern Ireland is included in Ireland, which is not a part of the United Kingdom.

Source: Immigration and Naturalization Service, *1985 Statistical Yearbook of the Immigration and Naturalization Service*, Table IMM1.2, 1986.

Recent Legal Immigration:
15 Largest Contributors 1981 to 1985

Rank	Country*	Total Number 1981-85	Rank	Country*	Total Number 1985
1	Mexico	335,563	1	Mexico	61,290
2	Philippines	230,542	2	Philippines	53,137
3	Vietnam	211,914	3	Korea	34,791
4	China**	167,466	4	China**	33,095
5	Korea	165,054	5	India	24,536
6	India	116,864	6	Dominican Republic	23,861
7	Dominican Republic	104,797	7	Vietnam	20,367
8	Jamaica	99,089	8	Jamaica	18,277
9	Laos	87,014	9	Thailand	17,577
10	United Kingdom***	76,473	10	Cuba	17,115
11	Canada and Newfoundland	65,380	11	Canada and Newfoundland	16,354
12	Cambodia	56,106	12	United Kingdom***	15,591
13	Iran	56,040	13	Iran	12,327
14	Colombia	51,300	14	Colombia	11,802
15	Cuba	50,859	15	Hong Kong	10,795

*Data for 1980 to 1983 refer to country of birth. Data for 1984 and 1985 refer to country of last permanent residence.

**Includes Taiwan.

***United Kingdom refers to England, Scotland, Wales and Northern Ireland.

Source: Immigration and Naturalization Service, *1985 Statistical Yearbook of the Immigration and Naturalization Service,* Table IMM1.2, 1986.

States Most Favored by Recent Immigrants as Intended Residence: Fiscal Years 1976 to 1979 and 1982 to 1986

Rank	State*	Total Number of Immigrants	
		FY1976-79**	FY1982-86**
1	California	477,700	762,255
2	New York	389,498	500,213
3	Texas	129,131	222,570
4	Florida	155,206	169,655
5	New Jersey	123,647	146,652
6	Illinois	112,881	139,178
7	Massachusetts	56,377	67,395
8	Pennsylvania	44,462	54,495
9	Virginia	33,194	53,425
10	Washington	29,524	53,387
11	Maryland	33,467	50,380
12	Michigan	43,801	43,250
13	Hawaii	35,493	40,338
14	Connecticut	30,393	35,404
15	Ohio	31,305	34,378

*Ranked according to the number of immigrants between 1982-1986.
**FY = Fiscal Year. It is the 12-month period beginning October 1 and running through September 30.

Note: State of intended residence was not available in FY1980 and FY1981.

Sources: For FY1976 to FY1979 and FY1982 to FY1985, Immigration and Naturalization Service, *1985 Statistical Yearbook of the Immigration and Naturalization Service,* Table IMM 5.2, 1986; for FY1986, unpublished data of the Immigration and Naturalization Service, Detail Run 423, 1987.

Percent of Population Growth Attributable to Immigration: 1901 to 1985

Period	Immigration Component of Total Population Growth (%)
1901-10	39.6
1911-20	17.7
1921-30	15.0
1930-34	-0.1
1935-39	3.2
1940-44	7.4
1945-49	10.2
1950-54	10.6
1955-59	10.7
1960-64	12.5
1965-69	19.7
1970-74	16.2
1975-79	19.5
1980-85*	28.4

*Data for 1980 to 1985 include an allowance of 200,000 per year for net illegal immigration, not included in earlier data. Estimated legal emigration is assumed to be 160,000 a year, increased from 36,000 a year for earlier data.

Source: Leon F. Bouvier and Robert W. Gardner, "Immigration to the U.S.: The Unfinished Story," *Population Bulletin*, The Population Reference Bureau, Vol. 41, No. 4, Table 6, November 1986.

Illegal Aliens Apprehended: Fiscal Years 1977 to 1987

Fiscal Year*	Aliens Apprehended
FY1977	1,042,215
FY1978	1,057,977
FY1979	1,076,418
FY1980	910,361
FY1981	975,780
FY1982	970,246
FY1983	1,251,357
FY1984	1,246,981
FY1985	1,348,749
FY1986	1,767,400
FY1987	1,190,488

*FY = Fiscal Year. It is the 12-month period beginning October 1 and running through September 30.

Sources: For FY1977 to FY1985, Immigration and Naturalization Service, *1985 Statistical Yearbook of the Immigration and Naturalization Service,* Table ENF 1.1, 1986; for FY1986 and FY 1987, the Immigration and Naturalization Service, 1987 and 1988.

Chapter 4

Young and Old Alike:
Births, Deaths, Age and Longevity

Births − Deaths = Natural Increase
Life Expectancy
The Aging of America
Age Distribution and the
        "Dependent" Population

Young and Old Alike:
Births, Deaths, Age and Longevity

Increased life expectancy and the 1946 to 1964 baby boom profoundly affect natural increases in our nation's population, as well as its age composition. In 1986, the life expectancy of Americans was nearly 75 years, the highest it has ever been. The median age also continues to climb and is now double what it was less than 200 years ago.

Births − Deaths = Natural Increase

The U.S. population grows by more than 2.3 million each year, according to Census Bureau reports, although other estimates suggest that annual growth may be as high as 3 million. More than 1.6 million people are added through natural increase, defined as the surplus of births over deaths (page 47). The remainder of our nation's population growth is contributed by immigrants who enter the country both legally (about 600,000 people each year) and illegally (estimates ranged from 200,000 to 1.5 million yearly before the implementation of 1986 immigration-reform legislation).

Both the *number* of people added through natural increase and the *rate* of natural increase have remained fairly constant since the end of the baby boom in 1964.

The number of live births in 1986, 3.7 million, was slightly fewer than the number reported for 1985, but more than any other year since 1970. More than 2 million Americans died in 1986, 15,000 more than in the previous year and the largest number ever reported for the United States. This large number is attributed to increases in the overall size of the population, especially in the numbers of people age 65 and over.

Life Expectancy

Life expectancy is at its highest point ever. A child born in 1986 is expected to live to be 74.9 years old, 20 years longer than a child born in 1920 (page 48).

The gap between the life expectancy of men and women widened dramatically for 50 years after 1920, from less than a year to 7.6 years. Since 1970, however, the gap has narrowed to 7 years.

Minority women and men, whose lives historically have been shortened by poverty, inadequate nutrition and a lack of access to health care, are slowly beginning to catch up to their white counterparts. The life expectancy of nonwhite women has narrowed to within 3.8 years of that of white women, and nonwhite men's life expectancy has moved to within 4.4 years of white men.

Overall gains in life expectancy are attributed to the development of antibiotics, improvements in infant mortality rates, a reduction in fatal heart disease caused by cigarette smoking and other health-damaging behavior and increases in access to and use of health care services.

The Aging of America

The median age of the U.S. population has doubled, from 16 in 1800 (the first year such records were kept) to 31.8 in 1986 (page 49). This dramatic rise is primarily attributed to increases in life expectancy. A minor reversal was caused by the baby boom, but with the aging of the baby-boom generation, the median age is projected to increase. By the year 2000, it is projected to be 5.7 years older than in 1982. By 2080, the median age of the U.S. population is expected to be almost 43.

Age Distribution and the 'Dependent' Population

As the large baby-boom generation moves through life, its impact on the age composition of the U.S. population will continue to be substantial, reducing the number of people in the 15-to-34 age bracket and increasing the ranks of those age 35 and older (page 50).

Despite the aging of the baby-boom generation, the percentage of people considered "dependent" (those under 18 plus those over 64) has changed relatively little. This is primarily because the increase in the proportion of older people has been countered by an overall decrease in the proportion of children in the population (page 52).

Although some population observers have voiced concern that American taxpayers will be forced to support an ever-greater number of dependents in the future, the U.S. Census Bureau projects that by 2010 the ratio of dependents to others in the population will be the lowest since World War II. In fact, the percentage of dependents at both ends of the age scale is expected to be only slightly higher by 2010 than the percentage of *child* dependents in the 1960s.

In 2030, however, the percentage of elderly dependents is projected to rise dramatically as the youngest members of the baby-boom generation hit 65. For the first time in history, the percentage of elderly dependents will equal that of child dependents. After 2030, the percentage of elderly dependents is expected to increase, while the percentage of child dependents will decrease a bit and then level out.

The percentage of those over 65 who are 85 and over is projected to skyrocket from 9.6% of the population in 1986 to 23.8% in 2050, as the youngest baby boomers reach 85.

Live Births, Deaths and Natural Increase: 1940 to 1986

(Numbers in thousands)

Natural increase is the surplus of births over deaths in a given year. (Births − deaths = natural increase.)
Birth rate is the number of live births per thousand population in a given year.
Death rate is the number of deaths per thousand population in a given year.

Year	Births		Deaths		Natural Increase	
	Number	Rate	Number	Rate	Number	Rate
1940	2,559	19.4	1,417	10.8	1,142	8.6
1950	3,632	24.1	1,452	9.6	2,180	14.5
1960	4,258	23.7	1,712	9.5	2,546	14.2
1970	3,731	18.4	1,921	9.5	1,810	8.9
1971	3,556	17.2	1,928	9.3	1,628	7.9
1972	3,258	15.6	1,964	9.4	1,294	6.2
1973	3,137	14.8	1,973	9.3	1,164	5.5
1974	3,160	14.8	1,934	9.1	1,226	5.7
1975	3,144	14.6	1,893	8.8	1,251	5.8
1976	3,168	14.6	1,909	8.8	1,259	5.8
1977	3,327	15.1	1,900	8.6	1,427	6.5
1978	3,333	15.0	1,928	8.7	1,405	6.3
1979	3,494	15.6	1,914	8.5	1,580	7.1
1980	3,612	15.9	1,990	8.8	1,622	7.1
1981	3,629	15.8	1,978	8.6	1,651	7.2
1982	3,681	15.9	1,975	8.5	1,706	7.4
1983	3,639	15.5	2,019	8.6	1,620	6.9
1984	3,669	15.5	2,039	8.6	1,630	6.9
1985	3,761	15.8	2,086	8.7	1,675	7.1
1986*	3,731	15.5	2,099	8.7	1,632	6.8

*Provisional Data

Sources: National Center for Health Statistics, *Monthly Vital Statistics Report*, Vol. 34 No. 6, September 26, 1985; Vol. 35, No. 13, August 24, 1987; Vol. 36, No. 5, August 28, 1987; ZPG calculations.

Life Expectancy At Birth:
1920 to 2080

Year	Total: All	Male	Female	White: All	Male	Female	Nonwhite: All	Male	Female
1920	54.1	53.6	54.6	54.9	54.4	55.6	45.3	45.5	45.2
1930	57.9	58.1	61.6	61.4	59.7	63.5	48.1	47.3	49.2
1940	62.9	60.8	65.2	64.2	62.1	66.6	53.1	51.5	54.9
1950	68.2	65.6	71.1	69.1	66.5	72.2	60.8	59.1	62.9
1960	69.7	66.6	73.1	70.6	67.4	74.1	63.6	61.1	66.3
1970	70.8	67.1	74.7	71.7	68.0	75.6	65.3	61.3	69.4
1980	73.7	70.0	77.4	74.4	70.7	78.1	69.5	65.3	73.6
1981	74.2	70.4	77.8	74.8	71.1	78.4	70.3	66.1	74.4
1982	74.5	70.9	78.1	75.1	71.5	78.7	71.0	66.8	75.0
1983	74.6	71.0	78.1	75.2	71.7	78.7	71.1	67.2	74.9
1984	74.7	71.2	78.2	75.3	71.8	78.8	71.3	67.3	75.2
1985*	74.7	71.2	78.2	75.3	71.8	78.7	71.2	67.2	75.2
1986*	74.9	71.3	78.3	75.4	72.0	78.9	71.4	67.6	75.1
Projections:							**Blacks Only****		
1990	n/a	71.6	79.2	n/a	72.4	79.7	n/a	66.3	75.4
2000	n/a	72.9	80.5	n/a	73.6	81.0	n/a	68.5	77.6
2020	n/a	74.2	82.0	n/a	74.7	82.3	n/a	71.0	79.9
2040	n/a	75.0	83.1	n/a	75.4	83.3	n/a	72.8	81.7
2060	n/a	75.9	84.1	n/a	76.1	84.2	n/a	74.8	83.4
2080	n/a	76.7	85.2	n/a	76.7	85.2	n/a	76.7	85.2

n/a = not available.

*Estimated.
**Numbers include blacks only. Data for other nonwhites not available.

Sources: For 1920 to 1940, National Center for Health Statistics (NCHS), as cited by U.S. Bureau of the Census, *Statistical Abstract of the United States 1987,* Table 105, 1986; for 1950 to 1986, NCHS, *Monthly Vital Statistics Report,* Vol. 35, No. 13, August 24, 1987; for 1990 to 2080, U.S. Bureau of the Census, "Projections of the Population of the United States, by Age, Sex, and Race: 1983 to 2080," *Current Population Reports,* Series P-25, No. 952, Table B-5, 1984.

Median Age of Population: 1800 to 2080

Median age is the age at which half of the population is younger and half is older.

Year	Age in Years	Year	Age in Years
1800*	16.0	1970	27.9
1810*	16.0	1980	30.0
1820	16.7	– – – – – – – – – – – – – –	
1830	17.2	1981	30.3
1840	17.8	1982	30.6
1850	18.9	1983	30.9
1860	19.4	1984	31.2
1870	20.2	1985	31.5
1880	20.9	1986	31.8
1890	22.0	– – – – – – – – – – – – – –	
1900	22.9	**Projections:**	
1910	24.1	1990	33.0
1920	25.3	2000	36.3
1930	26.5	2020	39.3
1940	29.0	2040	41.6
1950	30.2	2060	42.1
1960	29.4	2080	42.8

*Numbers include whites only.

Source: For 1800 to 1950, U.S. Bureau of the Census, *Historical Statistics of the United States, Colonial Times to 1970,* Part 1, Series A143–157, 1975; for 1960 to 1986, U.S. Bureau of the Census, "Estimates of the Population of the United States, by Age, Sex, and Race: 1980 to 1986," *Current Population Reports,* Series P-25, No. 1000, Table B, 1987; for 1990 to 2080, U.S. Bureau of the Census, "Projections of the Population of the United States, by Age, Sex, and Race: 1983 to 2080," *Current Population Reports,* Series P25, No. 952, Table 6, 1984.

Age Distribution: 1900 to 2000
(Numbers in thousands)

	1900		1920	
	Number	**Percent**	**Number**	**Percent**
All Ages	76,094	100.0	106,461	100.0
Under 5	9,181	12.1	11,631	10.9
5-14	16,966	22.3	22,158	20.8
15-24	14,951	19.7	18,821	17.7
25-34	12,161	16.0	17,416	16.4
35-44	9,273	12.2	14,382	13.5
45-54	6,437	8.5	10,505	9.9
55-64	4,026	5.3	6,619	6.2
65 and Over	3,099	4.1	4,929	4.6

	1940		1960	
	Number	**Percent**	**Number**	**Percent**
All Ages	132,122	100.0	180,671	100.0
Under 5	10,579	8.0	20,341	11.3
5-14	22,363	16.9	35,735	19.8
15-24	24,033	18.2	24,576	13.6
25-34	21,446	16.2	22,919	12.7
35-44	18,422	13.9	22,221	13.4
45-54	15,555	11.8	20,578	11.4
55-64	10,694	8.1	15,625	8.6
65 and Over	9,031	6.8	16,675	9.2

Continued, next page

Age Distribution: 1900 to 2000 (Cont.)

(Numbers in thousands)

	1980		1986	
	Number	Percent	Number	Percent
All Ages	227,757	100.0	241,596	100.0
Under 5	16,458	7.2	18,128	7.5
5-14	34,845	15.3	33,855	14.0
15-24	42,743	18.8	39,261	16.3
25-34	37,626	16.5	42,984	17.8
35-44	25,868	11.4	33,142	13.7
45-54	22,754	10.0	22,823	9.4
55-64	21,761	9.6	22,230	9.2
65 and Over	25,704	11.3	29,173	12.1

	2000 (Projections)	
	Number	Percent
All Ages	267,955	100.0
Under 5	17,626	6.6
5-14	38,277	14.3
15-24	36,088	13.5
25-34	36,415	13.6
35-44	43,743	16.3
45-54	37,119	13.9
55-64	23,767	8.9
65 and Over	34,921	13.0

Notes: 1900 to 1920 is resident population; 1940 to 2000 is total population including armed forces and nationals overseas.

Sources: For 1900 to 1960, U.S. Bureau of the Census, *Historical Statistics of the United States from Colonial Times to 1970,* Vol. 1, Series 29-42, 1975; for 1980 and 1986, U.S. Bureau of the Census, "Estimates of the Population of the United States, by Age, Sex, and Race: 1980 to 1986," *Current Population Reports,* Series P-25, No. 1000, Table 1, 1987; for 2000, U.S. Bureau of the Census, "Projections of the Population of the United States, by Age, Sex, and Race: 1983 to 2080," *Current Population Reports,* Series P-25, No. 952, Table 6, 1984; ZPG calculations.

Percent of Americans Under Age 18 and 65 or Over: 1950 to 2080

Year	Under 18 + 65 and Over	Under 18	65 and Over	% of 65 and Over Who Are 85 and Over	Age of Baby Boomers
1950	39.1	31.0	8.1	4.8	0-4
1955	42.4	33.6	8.8	5.3	0-9
1960	44.9	35.7	9.2	5.6	0-14
1965	45.4	35.9	9.5	5.9	1-19
1970	43.9	34.1	9.8	7.1	6-24
1975	41.6	31.1	10.5	8.0	11-29
1980	39.2	27.9	11.3	8.8	16-34
1986	38.3	26.2	12.1	9.6	22-40
Projections:					
1990	38.5	25.8	12.7	10.5	26-44
1995	39.0	25.9	13.1	12.0	31-49
2000	38.1	25.1	13.0	14.1	36-54
2010	36.7	22.9	13.8	16.7	46-64
2030	42.8	21.6	21.2	13.3	66-84
2050	42.8	21.0	21.8	23.8	86-104
2080	43.8	20.3	23.5	24.9	106 +

Sources: For 1986, U.S. Bureau of the Census, "Estimates of the Population of the United States, by Age, Sex, and Race: 1980 to 1986," *Current Population Reports*, Series P-25, No. 1000, Table 1, 1987 and ZPG calculations; for the remaining years, U.S. Bureau of the Census, "Projections of the Population of the United States, by Age, Sex, and Race: 1983 to 2080," *Current Population Reports*, Series P-25, No. 952, Tables F and G, 1984 and ZPG calculations.

Chapter 5

Baby Talk: Fertility and Birth Rates, Infant Health and Contraceptive Use

Baby Talk: Fertility and Birth Rates, Infant Health and Contraceptive Use

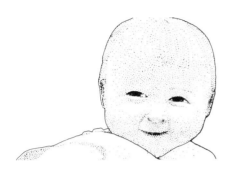

Health and quality of life are closely tied to long-range childbearing patterns. Improved education and income levels, and increased access to health care and effective contraceptives reduce fertility, birth and infant mortality rates and lower the incidence of low-birthweight babies. The U.S. lags behind most industrialized—and some developing—countries in reducing infant mortality rates and the chances of low-birthweight babies.

Trends in Fertility and Birth Rates

U.S. fertility and birth rates have declined steadily since the early 1900s, with the major exception of the mid-century baby boom (page 58). After 1964, both fertility and birth rates dropped below the historic lows of the 1930s, and have remained relatively constant since the mid-1970s.

In 1986, the fertility rate fell two points below 1985 levels, dropping to 64.9 live births per 1,000 women age 15 to 44, the lowest rate in more than 180 years.

Fertility rates among both white and nonwhite women have dropped dramatically over the past 25 years, by more than 44% for whites and by nearly 46% for nonwhites. Since 1975, fertility rates among nonwhite women have dropped by more than 5%, while white rates have held steady.

Despite dropping fertility *rates*, the actual *number* of annual live births has increased steadily for the past decade as the baby boomers generate their own baby "boomlet."

Smaller Families

The total fertility rate (the average number of children a woman is projected to bear during her lifetime) has been fairly constant for more than a decade (page 59).

Since 1972, the average number of children women are projected to have during their childbearing years has fluctuated below 2.1. Considered "replacement level," 2.1 is calculated as the number of children a couple must have in order to replace themselves. But although the total fertility rate is below replacement level, our nation's ever-expanding population base, a baby "boomlet" and large numbers of immigrants generate continuing population growth.

Fertility Rates by Race and Other Characteristics

The overall fertility rate of Hispanic women is significantly higher than that of other races (page 60). Although in 1986 only 8% of all women 18 to 44 were Hispanic, they accounted for 12% of total births.

Black women have higher fertility rates than white women, but not in all age groups. While black women 18 to 24 had dramatically higher fertility rates than their white counterparts in 1986, the rate for white women 25 to 29 was only slightly higher than that for black women in the same age group. Similarly, for women over 30, the two races' fertility rates are not substantially different.

Women who have not graduated from high school have a fertility rate almost 30 points higher than women with four or more years of college. Women not in the labor force have fertility rates more than twice that of women in the labor force. Women in families with incomes of less than $10,000 per year have fertility rates almost twice that of women whose families earn more than $35,000 per year. And women who live in the Midwest have a fertility rate almost 9 points lower than women who live in western states.

Infant Mortality Rates

U.S. infant mortality rates are among the highest in the industrialized world, and the nation has made little progress in reducing overall infant mortality in more than a decade. Thirty years ago, the United States ranked sixth best among 20 industrialized countries in infant mortality. By 1985, according to a study by the United Nation's Children's Fund, the U.S. had fallen into a tie for last place.

Almost 39,000 of the 3.7 million children born in the U.S. in 1986 died before their first birthday, a rate of 10.4 infant deaths per 1,000 live births (page 61).

Black infants have been dying at almost twice the rate of white babies for the past 30 years. In large cities like Indianapolis, Memphis, Philadelphia, Chicago and Cleveland, the infant mortality rate for blacks in 1984 was more than double that for whites (page 62). The *lowest* black infant mortality rate, in Columbus, Ohio, was virtually the same as the *highest* white infant mortality rate, in Detroit. Infant mortality rates also varied within states: a black infant born in Cleveland was almost twice as likely to die in the first year of life than one born in Columbus.

Low-Birthweight Babies

Statistics on low-birthweight infants are relevant because babies weighing less than 5.5 pounds at birth are 20 times more likely than babies born at normal weights to die before their first birthday.

The percentage of low-birthweight babies in the U.S. has declined less than 1% since 1950 (page 63). Nearly twice as many nonwhite infants are born at low birthweights than white infants, and the gap has widened in the past 20 years. Although just 16% of all newborns are black, nearly 30% of all low-birthweight babies are black.

A major contributor to the problem of low-birthweight infants is the high rate of births to teenagers, whose babies are far more likely than others to be born at low birthweights. Although teenage mothers account for almost 13% of all births, they are responsible for nearly 18% of all low-birthweight babies (page 64). Black infants born to teenage mothers are at significantly greater risk of low birthweight than white infants of teenagers.

Babies born to mothers age 25 to 34 have the least risk of low birthweight.

Contraceptive Use

More married and formerly married women chose sterilization than any other birth-control method in 1982, the latest year for which such statistics have been released (page 65). Although many married and formerly married women had abandoned oral contraceptives and IUDs in favor of less effective methods like condoms and diaphragms, the Pill still was their second contraceptive choice. The top three methods of birth control among women who have never been married were oral contraceptives, diaphragms and condoms, in that order.

Married women were twice as likely to use some form of contraception than unmarried and formerly married women. Fewer than 5% of sexually active married women who were not seeking pregnancy used no contraception. In contrast, more than 10% of never-married and formerly married, sexually active women who did not wish to become pregnant used no contraception at all.

Because of questions about the health risks posed by many contraceptive methods, the birth-control options available to American women are narrowing in this country, while they are expanding in most developing nations.

Fertility and Birth Rates: 1800 to 1986

Fertility rate constitutes the number of live births per thousand *women* age 15 to 44 years in a given year.
Birth rate constitutes the number of live births per thousand *population* in a given year.

Year	Fertility Rate: All	White	Nonwhite	Birth Rate: All	White	Nonwhite
1800	n/a	278.0	n/a	n/a	55.0	n/a
1850	n/a	194.0	n/a	n/a	43.3	n/a
1900	n/a	130.0	n/a	32.3	30.1	n/a
1920	117.9	115.4	137.5	27.7	26.9	35.0
1925	106.6	103.3	134.0	25.1	24.1	34.2
1930	89.2	87.1	105.9	21.3	20.6	27.5
1935	77.2	74.5	98.4	18.7	17.9	25.8
1940	79.9	77.1	102.4	19.4	18.6	26.7
1945	85.9	83.4	106.0	20.4	19.7	26.5
1950	106.2	102.3	137.3	24.1	23.0	33.3
1955	118.5	113.8	154.3	25.0	23.8	34.5
1960	118.0	113.2	153.6	23.7	22.7	32.1
1965	96.6	91.4	131.9	19.4	18.3	27.6
1970	87.9	84.1	113.0	18.4	17.4	25.1
1975	66.0	62.5	87.7	14.6	13.6	21.0
1976	65.0	61.5	85.8	14.6	13.6	20.8
1977	66.8	63.2	87.7	15.1	14.1	21.6
1978	65.5	61.7	87.0	15.0	14.0	21.6
1979	67.2	63.4	88.5	15.6	14.5	22.2
1980	68.4	64.7	88.6	15.9	14.9	22.5
1981	67.4	63.9	86.4	15.8	14.8	22.0
1982	67.3	63.9	85.5	15.9	14.9	21.9
1983	65.8	62.4	83.2	15.5	14.6	21.3
1984	65.4	62.2	82.5	15.5	14.5	21.2
1985	66.2	63.0	83.2	15.8	14.8	21.4
1986	64.9	n/a	n/a	15.5	n/a	n/a

n/a = not available.

Source: For 1800 to 1970, U.S. Bureau of the Census, *Historical Statistics of the United States from Colonial Times to 1970,* (Part 1), Series B5-10, 1975; for 1975 to 1986; National Center for Health Statistics, *Monthly Vital Statistics Report,* Vol. 35, No. 4, July 18, 1986; Vol. 35, No. 12, April 2, 1987 and Vol. 36, No. 4, July 17, 1987.

Total Fertility Rate: 1920 to 1985

Total fertility rate projects the average number of children a woman will have during her lifetime. The formal definition for total fertility rate is the number of live births that a woman would have during her lifetime if she experienced, through all her childbearing years, the age-specific birth rates of a given year.

Year	Total	White	Nonwhite
1920-1924	3.248	n/a	n/a
1925-1929	2.840	"	"
1930-1934	2.376	"	"
1935-1939	2.235	"	"
1940-1944	2.523	2.460	3.010
1945-1949	2.985	2.916	3.485
1950-1954	3.337	3.221	4.185
1955-1959	3.690	3.549	4.716
1960-1964	3.449	3.326	4.326
1965	2.913	2.783	3.808
1966	2.721	2.603	3.532
1967	2.558	2.447	3.299
1968	2.464	2.366	3.108
1969	2.456	2.360	3.061
1970	2.480	2.385	3.067
1971	2.267	2.161	2.920
1972	2.010	1.907	2.628
1973	1.879	1.783	2.444
1974	1.835	1.749	2.339
1975	1.774	1.686	2.276
1976	1.738	1.652	2.223
1977	1.790	1.703	2.278
1978	1.760	1.668	2.264
1979	1.808	1.715	2.310
1980	1.840	1.749	2.323
1981	1.815	1.726	2.275
1982	1.829	1.742	2.264
1983	1.803	1.718	2.225
1984	1.806	1.719	2.224
1985	1.843	1.754	2.263

n/a = not available.

Sources: For 1920 to 1939, U.S. Bureau of the Census, "Population of the United States, Trends and Prospects: 1950-1990," *Current Population Reports,* Series P-23, No. 49, Table 2.5, 1974; for 1940 to 1984, National Center for Health Statistics, *Vital Statistics of the United States* annual, as cited by U.S. Bureau of the Census in *Statistical Abstract of the United States 1987,* Table 81, 1986; for 1985, National Center for Health Statistics, *Monthly Vital Statistics Report,* Vol. 36, No. 4, July 17, 1987.

Fertility Rates of Women Ages 18 to 44: 1986

Characteristic	Total: Ages 18 to 44	Ages 18 to 24	Ages 25 to 29	Ages 30 to 44
Total, All Women	70.3	88.6	113.6	43.5
Race:				
White	68.2	83.1	112.7	43.2
Black	78.4	113.7	111.3	41.9
Hispanic	105.6	139.1	133.7	69.8
Other	67.3	83.7	111.7	41.5
Marital status:				
Currently married	95.3	198.6	154.1	52.8
Widowed or divorced	27.1	82.4	49.4	17.5
Single	32.1	36.9	35.0	13.7
Educational attainment:				
Not a high school graduate	93.1	149.0	128.9	40.9
High school, 4 years	71.0	103.0	128.8	30.7
College: 1 to 3 years	58.7	43.5	107.1	47.8
4 or more years	64.3	29.0	80.2	65.5
4 years	60.8	28.8	84.2	59.0
5 or more years	71.3	30.5	67.8	74.5
Labor force status:				
In labor force	48.5	54.9	80.6	32.1
Employed	46.5	50.5	78.0	32.0
Unemployed	74.1	84.4	110.8	32.7
Not in labor force	126.9	183.8	196.5	72.2
Family income:				
Under $10,000	95.3	141.6	109.3	49.2
$10,000 to $14,999	69.7	105.4	84.0	34.4
$15,000 to $19,999	69.3	101.6	105.1	32.4
$20,000 to $24,999	73.3	108.5	123.4	33.9
$25,000 to $29,000	75.4	79.2	130.9	50.1
$30,000 to $34,999	68.3	55.0	138.2	43.7
$35,000 and over	55.4	34.1	111.1	48.0
Income not reported	68.6	75.4	143.5	40.8
Region of residence:				
Northeast	67.4	66.0	114.4	50.2
Midwest	66.4	83.5	117.9	36.9
South	71.9	104.7	107.4	40.6
West	75.0	91.1	117.9	49.1

Note: **Fertility rate** here is slighty different than in the previous chart because it considers only women ages 18 to 44. The U.S. Bureau of the Census uses ages 18 to 44 to determine fertility rates, while other research organizations, like the National Center for Health Statistics, consider women ages 15 to 44.

Source: U.S. Bureau of the Census, "Fertility of American Women: June 1986," *Current Population Reports*, Series P-20, No. 421, Table A, 1987.

Infant Mortality Rates by Race: 1940 to 1986

Infant mortality rate indicates the number of deaths per thousand live births of infants younger than one year old in a given year.

Year	All Races	White	Nonwhite Black	Total	Ratio of Black to White
1940	47.0	43.2	72.9	73.8	1.69
1945	38.3	35.6	56.2	57.0	1.58
1950	29.2	26.8	43.9	44.5	1.64
1955	26.4	23.6	43.1	42.8	1.83
1960	26.0	22.9	44.3	43.2	1.93
1961	25.3	22.4	41.8	40.7	1.87
1962	25.3	22.3	42.6	41.4	1.91
1963	25.2	22.2	42.8	41.5	1.93
1964	24.8	21.6	42.3	41.1	1.96
1965	24.7	21.5	41.7	40.3	1.94
1966	23.7	20.6	40.2	38.8	1.95
1967	22.4	19.7	37.5	35.9	1.90
1968	21.8	19.2	36.2	34.5	1.89
1969	20.9	18.4	34.8	32.9	1.89
1970	20.0	17.8	32.6	30.9	1.83
1971	19.1	17.1	30.3	28.5	1.77
1972	18.5	16.4	29.6	27.7	1.80
1973	17.7	15.8	28.1	26.2	1.78
1974	16.7	14.8	26.8	24.9	1.81
1975	16.1	14.2	26.2	24.2	1.85
1976	15.2	13.3	25.5	23.5	1.92
1977	14.1	12.3	23.6	21.7	1.92
1978	13.8	12.0	23.1	21.1	1.93
1979	13.1	11.4	21.8	19.8	1.91
1980	12.6	11.0	21.4	19.1	1.95
1981	11.9	10.5	20.0	17.8	1.90
1982	11.5	10.1	19.6	17.3	1.94
1983	11.2	9.7	19.2	16.8	1.98
1984	10.8	9.4	18.4	16.1	1.96
1985	10.6	9.3	18.2	15.8	1.96
1986*	10.4	n/a	n/a	n/a	n/a

n/a = not available.

*Provisional data.

Note: Ratio indicates the number of black infant deaths for every one white infant.

Sources: For 1940 to 1984, National Center for Health Statistics, as cited by Children's Defense Fund in *Health of American's Children: Maternal and Child Health Data Book,* Table 3.1, 1987; for 1985 to 1986, National Center for Health Statistics, *Monthly Vital Statistics Report,* Vol. 35, No.12, April 2, 1987, and Vol. 36, No. 5, August 28, 1987.

Infant Mortality Rates for Cities
with Populations of 500,000 or More: 1984
(Ranked low to high by total infant mortality rates)

City	Total: Rank	Total: Rate	White: Rank	White: Rate	Nonwhite: Rank	Nonwhite: Rate	Black Only: Rank	Black Only: Rate
San Jose	1	7.9	3	8.3	*	*	*	*
San Francisco	2	8.8	4	8.5	1	9.0	*	*
Columbus	3	9.6	2	8.3	3	12.8	1	13.5
San Diego	4	9.7	5	8.8	2	11.9	7	18.1
Phoenix	5	9.9	9	9.4	*	*	*	*
Los Angeles	6	11.0	6	9.2	8	15.6	12	19.9
Boston	7	11.7	13	10.4	4	13.4	2	14.6
Dallas	8	11.7	11	9.7	7	15.2	4	15.7
Jacksonville	9	11.9	10	9.5	9	16.3	6	16.8
Houston	10	11.9	14	10.6	6	14.6	5	16.7
San Antonio	11	12.8	19	12.5	*	*	*	*
New York City	12	13.0	18	11.7	5	14.6	3	15.6
Indianapolis	13	13.3	8	9.4	18	23.6	18	24.5
Milwaukee	14	14.2	17	11.7	11	18.1	9	18.5
Memphis	15	14.8	1	7.8	13	19.2	11	19.3
Philadelphia	16	15.5	7	9.2	15	21.8	13	22.3
New Orleans	17	16.0	15	10.8	10	17.9	8	18.5
Chicago	18	16.5	16	11.1	14	21.5	14	22.6
Baltimore	19	16.8	20	13.2	12	18.5	10	18.7
Cleveland	20	16.8	12	10.2	16	23.0	15	23.2
Detroit	21	20.9	21	13.8	17	23.3	16	23.7
District of Columbia	22	21.0	*	*	19	24.1	17	24.3

*Not ranked because there were too few infant deaths to calculate a reliable rate.

Sources: National Center for Health Statistics and calculations by Children's Defense Fund as cited by Children's Defense Fund in *The Health of America's Children: Maternal and Child Health Data Book,* Tables 2.22A- 2.22D, 1987.

Percent of Low-Birthweight Babies: 1950 to 1985

A **low-birthweight baby** is one who is born weighing less than 5 pounds 8 ounces, or 2,500 grams.

Year	All Races	White	Nonwhite Black	Nonwhite Total	Ratio of Black to White
1950	7.5	7.1	n/a	10.2	n/a
1955	7.6	6.8	n/a	11.7	n/a
1960	7.7	6.8	n/a	12.8	n/a
1961	7.8	6.9	n/a	13.0	n/a
1962	8.0	7.0	n/a	13.1	n/a
1963	8.2	7.1	n/a	13.6	n/a
1964	8.2	7.1	n/a	13.9	n/a
1965	8.3	7.2	n/a	13.8	n/a
1966	8.3	7.2	n/a	13.9	n/a
1967	8.2	7.1	n/a	13.6	n/a
1968	8.2	7.1	n/a	13.7	n/a
1969	8.1	7.0	14.1	13.5	2.01
1970	7.9	6.8	13.9	13.3	2.04
1971	7.7	6.6	13.4	12.7	2.03
1972	7.7	6.5	13.6	12.9	2.09
1973	7.6	6.4	13.3	12.5	2.08
1974	7.4	6.3	13.1	12.4	2.08
1975	7.4	6.3	13.1	12.2	2.08
1976	7.3	6.1	13.0	12.1	2.13
1977	7.1	5.9	12.8	11.9	2.17
1978	7.1	5.9	12.8	11.9	2.17
1979	6.9	5.8	12.6	11.6	2.17
1980	6.8	5.7	12.5	11.5	2.19
1981	6.8	5.7	12.5	11.4	2.19
1982	6.8	5.6	12.4	11.2	2.21
1983	6.8	5.6	12.6	11.2	2.25
1984	6.7	5.6	12.4	11.1	2.21
1985	6.8	5.6	12.4	11.1	2.21

n/a = not available.

Sources: For 1950 to 1984, National Center for Health Statistics as cited by Children's Defense Fund in *The Health of America's Children: Maternal and Child Health Data Book,* Table 3.4, 1986; for 1985, National Center for Health Statistics, *Monthly Vital Statistics Report,* Vol. 36, No.4, July 17, 1987 and the National Center for Health Statistics' Natality Division, 1987.

Low-Birthweight Babies by Mother's Age and Child's Race: 1985

Mother's Age and Child's Race	Total Births	Low Birthweight	
		Number	Percent
All Races			
All Ages	**3,760,561**	**253,554**	**6.8**
Under 15 years	10,220	1,311	12.9
15 to 19 years	467,485	43,281	9.3
20 to 24 years	1,141,320	78,676	6.9
25 to 29 years	1,201,350	71,015	5.9
30 to 34 years	696,354	42,050	6.0
35 to 39 years	214,336	14,758	6.9
40 to 44 years	28,334	2,344	8.3
45 to 49 years	1,162	119	10.3
White			
All Ages	**2,991,373**	**168,390**	**5.6**
Under 15 years	4,101	428	10.5
15 to 19 years	318,725	24,319	7.6
20 to 24 years	894,195	51,333	5.7
25 to 29 years	997,233	49,958	5.0
30 to 34 years	580,398	30,193	5.2
35 to 39 years	173,681	10,459	6.0
40 to 44 years	22,264	1,633	7.3
45 to 49 years	776	67	8.7
Black			
All Ages	**608,193**	**75,414**	**12.4**
Under 15 years	5,860	863	14.8
15 to 19 years	134,270	17,893	13.3
20 to 24 years	207,330	24,902	12.0
25 to 29 years	152,306	18,221	12.0
30 to 34 years	78,129	9,661	12.4
35 to 39 years	26,216	3,318	12.7
40 to 44 years	3,888	520	13.4
45 to 49 years	194	36	18.8
Total Nonwhite			
All Ages	**769,188**	**85,164**	**11.1**
Under 15 years	6,119	883	14.5
15 to 19 years	148,760	18,962	12.8
20 to 24 years	247,125	27,343	11.1
25 to 29 years	204,117	21,057	10.3
30 to 34 years	115,956	11,857	10.2
35 to 39 years	40,655	4,299	10.6
40 to 44 years	6,070	711	11.7
45 to 49 years	386	52	13.6

Source: National Center for Health Statistics, *Monthly Vital Statistics Report*, Vol. 36, No.4, July 17, 1987.

Contraceptive Use by Marital Status and Contraceptive Method: 1982

Contraceptive Method	All Women	Never Married	Currently Married	Formerly Married
All Women (in thousands)	54,099	19,164	28,231	6,704
		Percent Distribution:		
Sterile:	27.2	3.2	40.9	38.0
Surgically sterile	25.7	2.6	38.9	36.1
Contraceptively sterile	17.8	1.8	27.8	21.6
Noncontraceptively sterile	7.8	.8	11.0	14.5
Nonsurgically sterile	1.5	.7	2.0	1.9
Nonsurgical contraceptors:	36.7	33.3	40.1	31.8
Pill	15.6	18.7	13.4	15.8
IUD	4.0	1.9	4.8	6.4
Diaphragm	4.5	4.7	4.5	3.7
Condom	6.7	4.1	9.8	.8
Foam	1.3	.4	2.0	1.1
Rhythm*	2.2	.9	3.2	1.4
Other methods**	2.5	2.6	2.3	2.7
Non-users:	36.1	63.4	18.9	30.3
Pregnant, post partum	5.0	2.5	7.2	2.6
Seeking pregnancy	4.2	1.2	6.7	2.1
Other nonusers	26.9	59.7	5.0	25.6
Not sexually active***	19.5	49.6	.2	15.1
Sexually active***	7.4	10.1	4.8	10.4

*Periodic abstinence and natural family planning.
**Withdrawal, douche, suppository and less frequently used methods.
***In the last three months before the survey.

Source: U.S. National Center for Health Statistics, as cited by the U.S. Bureau of the Census in *Statistical Abstract of the United States: 1986*, Table 100, 1985.

Chapter 6

Adolescent Sexuality and Pregnancy

Adolescent Sexuality and Pregnancy

The Alan Guttmacher Institute reported in 1985 that the U.S. has a higher incidence of adolescent pregnancy than any other developed nation, even though American teenagers are no more sexually active than adolescents elsewhere. While a high rate of teen pregnancy is not new in this country, recent studies show that economic and health consequences are far greater than previously realized.

Adolescent Sexuality

The proportion of sexually active, unmarried teenage girls increased dramatically between 1971 and 1982, from 30% to 45% (page 72). Virtually all of this increase was generated by whites. As a result, although black teenagers were still more sexually active than whites, the gap between the two had narrowed considerably.

By age 18, nearly three-quarters of unmarried black girls and more than half of their white counterparts had had sexual intercourse. The average age of first intercourse was 17.5 years for whites and 16.7 years for blacks.

Outcomes of Teen Pregnancies

Of the 1.1 million teens who became pregnant in 1983, 47% had live births, 40% had abortions and 13% miscarried (page 73). Pregnancy, birth and abortion rates were highest among teens age 18 and 19.

Births to Married and Unmarried Teens

Birth rates and numbers of births to all teenagers, married and unmarried combined, have been dropping slowly since 1970 (page 74). Black teenage birth rates remain more than twice that of whites, but the birth rate for black teens has declined more sharply than that for whites in the last 15 years.

While the number of births to and birth rates of *all* U.S. teenagers has been falling since 1970, both are on the rise among *unmarried* teens. Whites account for virtually the entire increase: both numbers and rates of births to single white teens are rising, while those of single black teens are falling.

Until 1980, the total number of black infants born each year to unmarried girls was actually higher than the number of white infants, even though unmarried, white teenage girls far outnumbered their black counterparts in the population. Only since 1981 has the number of white infants born to unmarried teenagers exceeded the number of black infants. Since then, the number of black infants born to unmarried mothers each year has decreased by almost 3,100, while the number has increased by 13,100 for whites.

In 1985, the rate of black births was 88.8 infants per 1,000 unmarried teenagers, while the rate of white births was 20.5 infants per 1,000 single mothers. Although the rate for blacks is still more than four times that for whites, the white rate is rising while the black rate is falling, narrowing the gap.

Teen Mothers in School

Whether or not a teenage girl returns to school after the birth of her first child depends to a great extent upon when and whether she marries, according to 1982 data (page 75). For both blacks and whites, teenage mothers who were not married when they gave birth were more likely than their married counterparts to return to school after childbirth, though black adolescents were more likely to return to school than whites.

When marriage took place between conception and childbirth, school enrollment six months after childbirth dropped for both blacks and whites, although the drop was more precipitous for blacks. Childbirth was much more likely to signal the end of white adolescents' education, no matter what their marital status.

Public Costs of Teenage Childbearing

Taxpayers spent nearly $18 billion in 1986 on food stamps, medical care and income supports for all families begun by teenage mothers, according to a study prepared by the Center for Population Options. This is a conservative calculation which does not include public funds spent for housing, special education, child care, foster care, child protective services and other social programs.

It is estimated that a family begun by a first birth to a teenage mother in 1986 will cost taxpayers $14,852 by the time that child reaches age 20 (page 76). Families begun by first births to adolescents in 1986 alone will cost taxpayers a total of $5.3 billion over the next 20 years.

The financial benefits of delayed adolescent childbearing are impressive. If the teenager who began her family in 1986 had waited until she was in her twenties to have her first child, taxpayers would save almost $6,000 instead of spending about $15,000 to support her family until that first child reached the age of 20. And if all 1986 births to teenagers had been delayed, taxpayers would save $2.1 billion over the next 20 years instead of spending $5.5 billion.

Adolescent Pregnancy, Birth and Abortion Rates by State

Adolescent pregnancy rates among the states vary widely, from 75 per 1,000 teenagers in North Dakota to 144 per 1,000 in Nevada, with 20 states rising above the national average of 111 (page 77). Birth rates range from a low of 28 per 1,000 adolescents in Massachusetts to a high of 84 in Mississippi, with half the states ranking above the national average of 53.

Abortion rates range from fewer than 15 per 1,000 teenage pregnancies in Utah to 69 in California, with 14 states reporting rates higher than the national average of 43. In California and Nevada, abortion rates are higher than birth and abortion rates combined in the two states which have the nation's lowest pregnancy rates (North Dakota and Minnesota).

Only a small number of states have both high birth rates *and* high abortion rates (Florida, Nevada and Texas), or low birth rates *and* low abortion rates (Iowa, Nebraska and North Dakota).

A 1986 study by the Alan Guttmacher Institute identified several factors which influence a state's teenage pregnancy, abortion and birth rates. The study found that race was relatively unimportant when other variables were considered.

For example, high *pregnancy* rates were found in states with high levels of population growth, residential mobility, crime, teenage suicide and poverty. For whites, high pregnancy rates were linked with a high percentage of children living in female-headed households and low pregnancy rates were found in states where a large proportion of senior high school students were enrolled in sex education classes.

High *birth* rates were reported by states with a large proportion of religious fundamentalists in the population and a large proportion of high-school dropouts. Low birth rates (and, generally, high abortion rates) were found in politically liberal states where women's status is relatively high, where a high proportion of women are served by family planning clinics, where Medicaid funding is available for abortions and where public education expenditures and teacher-student ratios are high. Contrary to popular myth, states with high maximum welfare payments had relatively low birth rates.

Adolescent Sexuality: 1971 to 1982

(Percent of teenage women who ever had premarital sexual intercourse)

Age	─────── Percent ───────			
	1971	1976	1979	1982
White and Black				
15 to 19	**30.4**	**43.4**	**49.8**	**44.9**
15	14.8	18.9	22.8	17.0
16	21.8	30.0	39.5	29.0
17	28.2	46.0	50.1	41.0
18	42.6	56.7	63.0	58.6
19	48.2	64.1	71.4	72.0
White Only				
15 to 19	**26.4**	**38.3**	**46.6**	**43.3**
15	11.8	14.2	18.5	15.4
16	17.8	25.2	37.4	27.3
17	23.2	40.0	45.8	39.4
18	38.8	52.1	60.3	56.3
19	43.8	59.2	68.0	70.4
Black Only				
15 to 19	**53.7**	**66.3**	**66.2**	**53.6**
15	31.2	38.9	41.7	24.8
16	46.4	55.1	50.9	37.6
17	58.4	71.9	74.6	49.4
18	62.4	78.4	77.0	73.6
19	76.2	85.3	88.7	81.4

Sources: For 1971, 1976 and 1979, National Surveys of Young Women (NSYW) and for 1982, National Survey of Family Growth–Cycle III (NSFG-III) as cited by Sandra L. Hofferth et al. in "Premarital Sexual Activity Among U.S. Teenage Women Over the Past Three Decades," *Family Planning Perspectives*, The Alan Guttmacher Institute, Vol. 19, No.2, Table 1, March/April 1987.

Teenage Pregnancies By Age and Outcome: 1983

(Rates per thousand women by age-specific group)

Age	All Pregnancies: Number	Rate*	Live Births: Number	Rate*	Induced Abortions: Number	Rate*	Estimated Miscarriages: Number	Rate*
Under 15	29,690	16.6	9,752	5.5	16,350	9.2	3,590	–
15 to 19	1,039,600	109.9	489,286	51.7	411,330	43.5	138,990	–
15 to 17	390,290	72.3	172,673	32.0	166,440	30.8	51,180	–
18 to 19	649,310	160.1	316,613	78.1	244,890	60.4	87,810	–
Total under 20	1,069,290	113.1	499,038	52.8	427,680	45.2	142,580	–

*The rate for under 15-year-olds is based on the population of women age 14. The rate for women under 20 is based on the population of women ages 15 to 19.

Notes: Miscarriages are estimated as 20% of births and 10% of abortions. Pregnancies are the sum of births, abortions and miscarriages.

Source: Alan Guttmacher Institute, unpublished data, 1987.

Births to Teenagers: 1940 to 1985

(Numbers in thousands)

Here, **birth rate** signifies the estimated number of live births per thousand women ages 15 to 19. The rate for *unmarried* women indicates the estimated number of live births per thousand unmarried women ages 15 to 19.

Date	All Births/ All Teens:		White		Nonwhite*		Black**	
	Number	Rate	Number	Rate	Number	Rate	Number	Rate
1940	332.7	53.4	246.9	45.6	85.8	109.5	n/a	n/a
1945	298.9	50.5	216.5	42.2	82.4	107.3	n/a	n/a
1950	432.9	79.4	324.9	69.3	108.0	145.0	n/a	n/a
1955	492.1	90.4	376.3	80.4	115.8	152.5	n/a	n/a
1960	593.1	91.0	461.3	82.5	131.8	146.6	n/a	n/a
1965	596.5	73.3	446.8	63.8	149.7	136.4	143.5	141.6
1970	651.3	69.7	467.0	59.0	184.3	133.4	174.9	138.1
1975	590.1	56.7	414.2	47.4	175.9	106.4	164.6	111.4
1980	552.2	53.0	388.1	44.7	164.1	94.6	150.4	100.0
1985	467.5	51.3	318.7	42.8	148.8	89.7	134.3	94.7

Date	All Births/ Unmarried Teens:		White		Nonwhite*		Black**	
	Number	Rate	Number	Rate	Number	Rate	Number	Rate
1940	40.5	7.4	16.0	3.3	24.5	42.5	n/a	n/a
1945	49.2	9.5	20.3	n/a	28.9	n/a	n/a	n/a
1950	56.0	12.6	19.9	5.1	36.1	68.5	n/a	n/a
1955	68.9	15.1	23.7	6.0	45.3	77.6	n/a	n/a
1960	87.1	15.3	32.8	6.6	54.3	76.5	n/a	n/a
1965	123.2	16.7	50.7	7.9	72.4	77.1	n/a	n/a
1970	190.4	22.4	79.3	10.9	111.1	90.8	107.8	96.9
1975	222.5	24.2	93.9	12.1	128.6	88.1	123.8	95.1
1980	262.8	27.6	128.0	16.2	134.8	81.7	128.0	89.2
1985	270.9	31.6	142.1	20.5	128.8	79.4	120.4	88.8

n/a = not available.

*Nonwhite data includes data for births of blacks.

**Data not available on births of blacks-only prior to 1964 or on unmarried black women prior to 1969.

Sources: For "All Births to Teens" 1940 to 1975, U.S. Bureau of the Census, *Current Population Reports,* "Projections of the Population of the United States, by Age, Sex and Race: 1983 to 2080," Series P-25, No. 952, Table A8-A10, 1984; for "All Births to Unmarried Teens" 1940 to 1975, National Center for Health Statistics (NCHS), *Trends and Differentials in Births to Unmarried Women: United States, 1970–1976,* Series C, No. 86, Tables 1 and 2, 1980; for 1980 to 1984, NCHS, *Monthly Vital Statistics Report,* Vol. 31, No. 8, November 30, 1982; Vol. 32, No. 9, December 29, 1983; Vol. 33, No. 6, September 28, 1984; Vol. 34, No. 6, September 20, 1985; Vol. 35, No. 4, July 18, 1986; Vol. 36, No. 4, July 17, 1987.

Teenage Mothers Who Return to School: 1982

Sequencing	Percent Enrolled 6 Months after Childbirth:		Percent Ever Enrolled after Childbirth:	
	White	Black	White	Black
Premarital birth	20.1	56.4	33.1	62.9
Premarital conception, postmarital birth	11.3	14.9	18.8	42.7
Postmarital conception	8.8	43.4	23.6	39.5

Sources: 1982 National Survey of Family Growth, as cited by S. McLaughlin et al., "The Effects of the Sequencing of Marriage and First Birth During Adolescence," *Family Planning Perspectives,* The Alan Guttmacher Institute, Vol. 18 No. 1, Tables 1 and 2, January/February 1986.

Public Costs of First Births and Potential Savings of Delayed Childbearing Among Teenagers: 1986
(Single cohort costs in billions)

Single birth costs reflects how much a family begun by a first birth in 1986 will cost taxpayers by the time the child reaches age 20.

Single cohort costs show how much the total number of families begun by teen first births in 1986 will cost over the next 20 years.

Single birth savings is the amount taxpayers would have saved if a baby had not been born while the mother was a teenager.

Single cohort savings is the amount that would have been saved if all teenage births in 1986 had been delayed.

Age at First Birth	Number of First Births*	Public costs		Savings**	
		Single Birth	Single Cohort	Single Birth	Single Cohort
All	**359,272**	**$14,852**	**$5.34**	**$5,941**	**$2.13**
Under 15	9,848	$18,913	$0.19	$7,565	$0.08
15 to 17	145,140	$18,897	$2.74	$7,559	$1.10
18 to 19	214,132	$11,984	$2.57	$4,794	$1.03

*1985 natality statistics are the latest available.
**Calculated at 40% of full cost.

Notes: Costs include public outlays for AFDC, Medicaid and food stamps, and *do not* include other services such as housing, special education, child protection services, foster care, day care, and other social services. Calculations are based on a 20-year projection, covering the years 1986 to 2005. Costs and saving are expressed in 1986 "present value" dollars, that is, the amount adjusted for inflation that would have to be set aside in 1986 to cover the 20-year cost of families begun by a first birth to a teen in 1986.

Sources: Center for Population Options, "Estimates of Public Costs for Teenage Childbearing, 1986 Report," Table 2, 1987; National Center for Health Statistics, *Monthly Vital Statistics Report*, Vol. 36, No. 4, July 17, 1987, and ZPG calculations.

Adolescent Pregnancy, Birth and Abortion Rates by State: 1980

(Rates per thousand women ages 15 to 19)

State	Pregnancy* Rate	Birth Rate	Abortion Rate
U.S. Total	**111.2**	**53.3**	**42.9**
Alabama**	117.3	68.3	32.2
Alaska**	124.2	64.4	42.7
Arizona	123.2	65.5	40.6
Arkansas	117.2	74.5	25.3
California	140.2	53.3	69.3
Colorado	113.7	49.9	48.0
Connecticut**	80.7	30.5	40.1
Delaware	105.6	51.2	40.1
Florida**	131.2	58.5	55.4
Georgia	130.9	71.9	40.5
Hawaii	105.6	50.7	40.7
Idaho	96.4	59.5	22.7
Illinois	100.6	55.8	30.6
Indiana	101.9	57.5	29.9
Iowa**	79.0	43.0	25.0
Kansas	101.0	56.8	29.8
Kentucky**	110.7	72.3	21.8
Louisiana	118.1	76.0	24.4
Maine	86.9	47.4	27.3
Maryland	122.5	43.4	64.0
Massachusetts	85.7	28.1	47.3
Michigan	102.4	45.0	44.0
Minnesota	77.0	35.4	31.4
Mississippi	125.0	83.7	22.3
Missouri	106.4	57.8	33.6
Montana	93.3	48.5	31.9
Nebraska	80.7	45.1	24.2
Nevada	144.0	58.5	67.1
New Hampshire**	80.7	33.6	36.7
New Jersey	95.8	35.2	48.7
New Mexico	125.6	71.8	35.8

Continued, next page

Adolescent Pregnancy,
Birth and Abortion Rates by State: 1980 (Cont.)
(Rates per thousand women ages 15 to 19)

State	Pregnancy* Rate	Birth Rate	Abortion Rate
U.S. Total	**111.2**	**53.3**	**42.9**
New York	100.7	34.8	53.6
North Carolina	110.3	57.5	37.5
North Dakota	74.8	41.7	22.5
Ohio	101.3	52.5	34.8
Oklahoma	119.5	74.6	27.3
Oregon	118.7	50.9	52.4
Pennsylvania	90.3	40.5	37.9
Rhode Island	83.1	33.0	39.6
South Carolina	113.7	64.8	32.7
South Dakota	86.4	52.6	21.2
Tennessee	113.0	64.1	32.8
Texas**	137.0	74.3	43.5
Utah	94.6	65.2	14.9
Vermont	94.8	39.5	43.1
Virginia	107.4	48.3	44.9
Washington	122.3	46.7	60.3
West Virginia**	103.6	67.8	20.2
Wisconsin**	84.8	39.5	34.0
Wyoming	126.6	78.7	29.2

*In order to take into account miscarriages and stillbirths, pregnancy rates are estimated as follows: (1.2 x birthrate) + (1.1 x abortion rate).

**Abortion data is estimated, based on the proportion of all abortions obtained by teenagers in similar states.

Source: Susheela Singh, "Adolescent Pregnancy in the United States: An Interstate Analysis," *Family Planning Perspectives*, The Alan Guttmacher Institute, Vol. 18, No. 5, Table 1, September/October 1986.

Chapter 7

Abortion in America

Availability of Legal Abortions
Abortion Numbers, Rates and Ratios
Abortion- and Birth-Related Maternal Mortality

Abortion In America

Although abortion is legal in the U.S., it is still financially and geographically beyond the reach of many women. Planned Parenthood reports that about 20,000 illegal abortions are still performed in this country each year, either self-induced or performed by non-licensed practitioners, and that the risk of death from illegal abortion can be 30 times greater than that of legal abortion.

Availability of Legal Abortions

A study by the Alan Guttmacher Institute reported that no abortion services were available in almost 82% of all U.S. counties in 1985, although more than 30% of all women of reproductive age lived in these counties. The proportion of counties with no abortion service providers actually increased by 4% from 1982 to 1985.

The study also noted that most states withhold state Medicaid funds from low-income women for abortion services and many service providers refuse to accept state Medicaid funds as payment for abortions performed. For many low-income women denied access to Medicaid-funded abortions, the cost—about $200 to $300 in 1986—is prohibitive.

Access to safe, legal abortion is further threatened by organized efforts to outlaw the procedure, by destruction of abortion facilities and by harassment of and violence against clinic staff members and clients. The cost of insuring clinics, staff and clients against property damage and personal injury has skyrocketed, forcing some clinics to close their doors.

Abortion Numbers, Rates and Ratios

After abortion was legalized in 1973, the number and rate of reported abortions increased dramatically (page 83). In the early 1980s, as pregnancy rates began to level off and then decline somewhat, abortion rates dropped proportionally. Nearly 1.6 million legal abortions were performed in 1985, a rate of about 28 abortions per 1,000 women age 15 to 44.

The abortion ratio, defined as the number of abortions per 100 pregnancies, rose rapidly from 19 in 1973 to 30 in 1980. The ratio stabilized for the next 5 years, dropping only slightly, to 29.8, in 1985.

In 1983, most women seeking abortions were young, white and unmarried (page 84). Young women 20 to 24 comprised the greatest percentage of all abortions performed (35%), followed by teenagers (27%). In contrast, less than 7% of all women who terminated their pregnancies were 35 and older.

White women had almost 70% of all abortions in 1983, although their abortion rate, 23 per 1,000 women, was less than half that of nonwhites. More than 80% of all abortions were obtained by unmarried women.

In the decade from 1973 to 1983, women over 34 and teenagers had the highest abortion ratios among women of childbearing age (page 85). In 1983, more than half of pregnancies among women 40 and older and almost half of pregnancies among girls under the age of 15 ended in abortion. The lowest abortion ratio was among women age 25 to 29.

Abortion- and Birth-Related Maternal Mortality

In 1970, when abortion was legal only in a handful of states and permitted only in extremely limited circumstances, more than 18 of every 100,000 pregnant women who risked abortion did not survive the procedure (page 86). This was the last year in which more women died from legal abortions than from childbirth.

Today, fewer than one woman dies for every 100,000 legal abortions performed. This dramatic decline is attributed primarily to the growing skill of physicians and to a shift from later to earlier abortions using safer procedures.

Death rates for women who carry their pregnancies to term have been halved since 1970, from 16 maternal deaths per 100,000 live births to 8. However, it is still 11 times more dangerous for a woman to carry a pregnancy to term than to terminate it through legal abortion.

Legal Abortion, Rates and Ratios: 1973 to 1985

Abortion rate is the estimated number of abortions per thousand women age 15 to 44 in a given year.

Abortion ratio is the number of abortions per hundred known pregnancies, or the percent of pregnancies not ending in miscarriage or stillbirth which end by abortion.

Year	Number (in thousands)	Abortion Rate	Abortion Ratio
1973*	744.6	16.3	19.3
1974	898.6	19.3	22.0
1975	1,034.2	21.7	24.9
1976	1,170.3	24.2	20.5
1977	1,316.7	26.4	28.6
1978	1,409.6	27.7	29.4
1979	1,497.7	28.8	29.7
1980	1,553.9	29.3	30.0
1981	1,577.3	29.3	30.1
1982	1,573.9	28.8	30.0
1983	1,575.0	28.5	30.4
1984	1,577.2	28.1	29.7
1985	1,588.6	28.0	29.8

*Abortion was legalized in 1973.

Source: S.K. Henshaw, J.D. Forrest, and J. Van Vort, "Abortion Services in the United States, 1984 and 1985," *Family Planning Perspectives,* The Alan Guttmacher Institute, Vol. 19 No. 2, Table 1, March/April 1987.

Abortions by Age, Race and Marital Status: 1983

Abortion rate here is the estimated number of abortions per thousand women of an age-specific group.
Percent distribution is the proportion of abortions performed on an age-specific group, based on the total number of abortions.

Characteristic	Number	Percent Distribution	Abortion Rate
Total	1,575,000	100.0	28.5
Age Group			
Under 15	16,350	1.0	9.1*
15 to 19	411,330	26.1	43.5
[15 to 17]	[166,440]	[10.6]	[30.8]
[18 to 19]	[244,890]	[15.5]	[60.4]
20 to 24	548,130	34.8	51.1
25 to 29	328,280	20.8	31.1
30 to 34	171,560	10.9	17.8
35 to 39	78,090	5.0	9.6
40 and older	21,260	1.4	3.1**
Race			
White	1,084,360	68.8	23.3
Nonwhite	490,640	31.2	55.8
Marital Status			
Married	294,670	18.7	10.3
Unmarried	1,280,330	81.3	48.1

*Rate per thousand 14-year-old girls.
**Rate per thousand women age 40 to 44.

Source: S.K. Henshaw, "Characteristics of U.S. Women Having Abortions, 1982-1983," *Family Planning Perspectives*, The Alan Guttmacher Institute, Vol. 19 No. 1, Tables 1 and 2, January/February, 1987.

Abortions by Age:
1973 to 1983

Percent distribution is the proportion of abortions performed on an age-specific group, based on the total number of abortions.

Abortion ratio is the number of abortions per hundred known pregnancies, or the percent of pregnancies not ending in miscarriage or stillbirth which end by abortion.

Age	─────── 1973 ─────── Number	Percent Distribution	Abortion Ratio	─────── 1977 ─────── Number	Percent Distribution	Abortion Ratio
Under 15	11,630	1.6	n/a	15,650	1.2	41.1
15 to 19	232,440	31.2	25.6*	396,630	30.1	38.3
[15 to 17]	[n/a]	[n/a]	[n/a]	[165,610]	[12.6]	[38.7]
[18 to 19]	[n/a]	[n/a]	[n/a]	[231,020]	[17.5]	[37.9]
20 to 24	240,610	32.3	17.6	449,660	34.2	27.6
25 to 29	129,600	17.4	13.2	246,680	18.7	20.2
30 to 34	72,550	9.7	18.7	124,380	9.4	23.7
35 to 39	40,960	5.5	28.3	61,700	4.7	38.5
40 and older	16,820	2.3	39.7	22,000	1.7	52.5

Age	─────── 1981 ─────── Number	Percent Distribution	Abortion Ratio	─────── 1983 ─────── Number	Percent Distribution	Abortion Ratio
Under 15	15,240	1.0	43.3	16,350	1.0	46.0
15 to 19	433,330	27.5	40.6	411,330	26.1	42.2
[15 to 17]	[175,932]	[11.2]	[41.7]	[166,440]	[10.6]	[43.2]
[18 to 19]	[257,398]	[16.3]	[39.9]	[244,890]	[15.5]	[41.4]
20 to 24	554,940	35.2	30.2	548,130	34.8	31.4
25 to 29	316,260	20.0	22.1	328,280	20.8	22.5
30 to 34	167,240	10.6	24.2	171,560	10.9	23.0
35 to 39	69,510	4.4	37.5	78,090	5.0	34.2
40 and older	20,820	1.3	51.1	21,260	1.4	51.4

n/a = not available.

*Ratio combines under 15 with 15 to 19.

Sources: For 1973 to 1981, S. K. Henshaw and Ellen Blaine, ed., *Abortion Services in the United States, Each State and Metropolitan Area, 1981-1982,* The Alan Guttmacher Institute, 1985; for 1983, S. K. Henshaw, "Characteristics of U.S. Women Having Abortions, 1982-1983," *Family Planning Perspectives,* The Alan Guttmacher Institute, Vol. 19, No. 1, Table 1 and 2, January/February 1987.

Abortion-Related and Birth-Related Maternal Mortality: 1970 to 1983

Year	Deaths per 100,000 Legal Abortions*	Deaths per 100,000 Live Births**
1970	18.6	16.4
1971	11.1	14.3
1972	4.1	15.2
1973	3.4	12.6
1974	2.8	12.1
1975	2.8	10.3
1976	0.9	10.6
1977	1.3	9.3
1978	0.5	8.0
1979	1.2	7.9
1980	0.5	7.5
1981	0.5	8.5
1982	0.8	7.9
1983	0.7	8.0

*For 1970 and 1971, estimates from data reported by the National Center for Health Statistics (NCHS). For 1972 to 1983, based on numbers of deaths reported by the Centers for Disease Control.

**Based on numbers of deaths reported by the NCHS.

Sources: For 1970 to 1980, C. Tietze, "The Public Health Effects of Legal Abortion in the United States," *Family Planning Perspectives,* The Alan Guttmacher Institute, Vol. 16 No. 1, Table 1, January/February 1984; for 1981 to 1983 abortion mortality rates, Centers for Disease Control, Abortion Statistics Division, March 1987; for 1981 to 1983 death rates, National Center for Health Statistics, *Monthly Vital Statistics Reports,* Vol. 31, No. 13, October 5, 1983; Vol. 33, No. 3, June 22, 1984; Vol. 34, No. 6, September 26, 1985.

Chapter 8

The U.S. Labor Force: On the Job and Out of Work

The U.S. Labor Force:
On the Job and Out of Work

The fortunes of millions of American workers are influenced by population-linked trends, including the baby-boom generation's move through the labor force and thousands of citizens' migration to Sunbelt states. The lowest unemployment rate in over a decade has not raised those fortunes evenly throughout the nation's work force or geographical regions.

Labor Force and Unemployment Rates

Over the past 50 years, the nation's unemployment rate has swung from a high of 20% in 1935 to a low of just under 2% in 1945 (page 92). After reaching a post-war high of 9.7% in 1982, the unemployment rate fell in 1986 to just under 7% for the first time since the mid-1970s. At the end of 1987, more than 7 million Americans were unemployed.

Employment growth began to slow in the late 1970s. While the size of the labor force grew by an average of more than 2.6 million annually between 1975 and 1980, only 1.7 million workers were added to the labor force each year, on average, for the next five years. This slowdown is primarily a reflection of the movement of the baby boomers from their entry into the labor force through their prime working years.

Working Men and Women

Men's rates of participation in the labor force are higher than women's in all age groups (page 93). Although the gap between the two is diminishing, it is expected to continue at least through the next decade.

The numbers of both men and women in the "prime age" category (those between 25 and 54) will comprise a greater and greater share of the total work force as the baby-boom generation matures. By 2000, it is projected that about three-quarters of the labor force will be in the 25-to-54 age group, as the youngest baby boomers turn 36 and the oldest celebrate their 54th birthdays.

During the years from 1972 through 1986, women between the ages of 25 and 54 comprised the fastest-growing group in the labor force, adding 16 million people. The number of men in this age group grew steadily as well: 11.3 million were added to the labor force during the same period.

Younger and Older Workers

The youth labor force expanded rapidly during the 1970s, leveled off by the mid-1980s, and is expected to decline in absolute numbers over the next decade, reflecting the movement of baby boomers out of the "young worker" category (page 93). The negative impact on some employment sectors of a decline in the numbers of younger workers is expected to be offset by an increase in the numbers of women and minorities entering the work force.

The numbers of older people in the labor force also expanded in the decade between 1975 and 1984 before it stabilized. The participation rate of older workers is projected to drop over the next decade as more and more people take early retirement and are covered by pension plans.

Minorities in the Work Force

Minorities are gradually increasing their share of participation in the work force (page 93). Between 1972 and 1986, more than 3.9 million blacks were added to the ranks, an increase of 45%. Combined, blacks, Hispanics, Asians and other race groups will account for roughly 57% of labor-force growth from 1986 to the year 2000.

Unemployment by Race

Unemployment rates for whites and nonwhites have dropped substantially since they hit post-war highs in 1982 and 1983 (page 94). Although the gap between whites and nonwhites narrowed slightly in the late 1960s, the unemployment rate for nonwhites generally has been double that for whites since the early 1950s.

Since the government first began to record black and Hispanic unemployment rates in the early 1970s, black rates have ranged between 2 and 6 points higher than those of Hispanics. The narrowest gap occurred in 1973, the widest a decade later.

Youth Unemployment by Race

For young people age 16 to 19 who are looking for work (including summer jobs and part-time work), unemployment rates are dramatically higher than those for adults (page 95). The early 1980s marked a period of soaring unemployment for white, black and Hispanic youths, when 20% of whites, 48% of blacks and 30% of Hispanics were out of work.

The gap between white and black unemployment rates was narrowest in 1973 and widest in 1983. For Hispanics, the gap between their unemployment rates and those of whites was at its narrowest in 1979 and widest in 1982.

Although youth unemployment rates have dropped almost 5 points since 1983 for whites and Hispanics and almost 9 points for blacks, they are still high: in 1987, 14.4% of white youths, 22.3% of Hispanic teenagers and 34.7% of black young people were unable to find jobs.

State Unemployment Rates

In 1986, a year when the nation's unemployment rate dropped below 7% for the first time in more than a decade, eight states posted unemployment rates above 9%, while 12 states reported rates of 5% and below (page 96).

The drop in global oil prices, the ensuing loss of oil-linked jobs and a slump in U.S. auto sales boosted both unemployment rates and the numbers of unemployed people in several states. Michigan, Louisiana and Texas ranked among both the 10 states with the largest numbers of unemployed people and the states with the highest unemployment rates.

While Alabama and Wyoming both had unemployment rates which put them in the worst-10 list, they also were among the states with the fewest numbers of unemployed people.

Five New England states with fairly stable populations were among the nine states with the lowest unemployment rates, four of which had rates of 4% or less: Connecticut, Massachusetts, New Hampshire and Rhode Island. New Hampshire's unemployment rate–2.8%–was the nation's lowest. A combined total of 160,000 people were unemployed in these four states.

However, in booming Sunbelt states like California and Florida, where population growth is outpacing economic growth, hundreds of thousands of people were out of work. In California alone, more than 890,000 people could not find jobs, a number larger than the combined total of unemployed workers in 20 other states, including three with the nation's worst unemployment rates.

Labor Force and Unemployment Rates:
1900 to 1987
(Numbers in thousands*)

The **labor force** represents the resident population, less the armed forces, who are employed either full- or part-time and who are seeking employment.

The **unemployment rate** is the percent of people in the total labor force who are seeking employment. The rate does not cover those who are employed part-time but seeking full-time work nor those who searched for employment unsuccessfully for some time but eventually dropped out of the labor force.

Year	Total Labor Force	Employed	Unemployed	Unemployment Rate (Percent)
1900	28,376	26,956	1,420	5.0
1905	32,299	30,918	1,381	4.3
1910	36,709	34,559	2,150	5.9
1915	39,600	36,223	3,377	8.5
1920	41,340	39,208	2,132	5.2
1925	45,169	43,716	1,453	3.2
1930	48,523	44,183	4,340	8.9
1935	52,283	41,673	10,610	20.3
1940	55,640	47,520	8,120	14.6
1945	53,860	52,820	1,040	1.9
1950	62,208	58,920	3,288	5.3
1955	65,023	62,171	2,852	4.4
1960	69,628	65,778	3,852	5.5
1965	74,455	71,088	3,366	4.5
1970	82,715	78,627	4,088	4.9
1975	93,775	85,846	7,929	8.5
1980	106,940	99,303	7,637	7.1
1981	108,670	100,397	8,273	7.6
1982	110,204	99,526	10,678	9.7
1983	111,550	100,834	10,717	9.6
1984	113,544	105,005	8,539	7.5
1985	115,462	107,150	8,312	7.2
1986	117,834	109,597	8,237	6.9
1987	119,865	112,440	7,425	6.2

*Numbers are annual averages reported in thousands of persons age 16 and over except prior to 1947, age 14 and over.

Sources: For 1900 to 1970, U.S. Bureau of the Census, *Historical Statistics of the United States, Colonial Times to 1970,* Part 1, Tables D1-10, D11-25, and D85-86, 1975; for 1975 to 1984, U.S. Bureau of Labor Statistics, as cited by the U.S. Bureau of the Census, *Statistical Abstract of the United States 1986,* Table 659, 1985; for 1985, 1986 and 1987, U.S. Department of Labor, Bureau of Labor Statistics, 1988.

Labor Force by Sex, Age, and Race:
1972 to 1986 and Projections to 2000
(Numbers in thousands)

Group	Actual 1972 Number	Actual 1972 Percent	Actual 1986 Number	Actual 1986 Percent	Percent Change 1972 to 1986	Projected 2000 Number	Projected 2000 Percent	Percent Change 1986 to 2000
Total, 16 and over	87,037	100.0	117,837	100.0	35.4	138,775	100.0	17.8
Men	53,556	61.5	65,423	55.5	22.2	73,136	52.7	11.8
16 to 24	11,243	12.9	12,251	10.4	9.0	11,506	8.3	-6.1
25 to 54	33,133	38.1	44,406	37.7	34.0	53,024	38.2	19.4
55 and over	9,180	10.5	8,766	7.4	-4.5	8,606	6.2	-1.8
Women	33,481	38.5	52,414	44.5	56.5	65,639	47.3	25.2
16 to 24	8,943	10.3	11,117	9.4	24.3	11,125	8.0	0.1
25 to 54	19,192	22.1	35,159	29.8	83.2	47,756	34.4	35.8
55 and over	5,346	6.1	6,138	5.2	14.8	6,758	4.9	10.1
White	77,275	88.8	101,801	86.4	31.7	116,701	84.1	14.6
Black	8,748	10.1	12,684	10.8	45.0	16,334	11.8	28.8
Asian and other*	n/a	n/a	3,352	2.8	n/a	5,740	4.1	71.2
Hispanic**	n/a	n/a	8,076	6.9	n/a	14,086	10.2	74.4

n/a = not available.

*The "Asian and other" group includes Native Americans including Alaskan Natives, Asians and Pacific Islanders. Labor force data for Asians and other are not available for 1972.

**Persons of Hispanic origin may be of any race. Labor force data for Hispanics not available before 1976.

Source: U.S. Department of Labor, Bureau of Labor Statistics, *U.S. Department of Labor News,* USDL 78-258, Table 1, June 25, 1987.

Unemployment Rates by Race: 1950 to 1987

The **unemployment rate** is the percent of people in the total labor force who are seeking employment. The rate does not include those who are employed part-time but seeking full-time work nor those who searched for employment unsuccessfully for some time and eventually dropped out of the labor force.

Year	White	Total Nonwhite	Black	Hispanic
1950	4.9	9.0	n/a	n/a
1955	3.9	8.7	n/a	n/a
1960	4.9	10.2	n/a	n/a
1961	6.0	12.4	n/a	n/a
1962	4.9	10.9	n/a	n/a
1963	5.0	10.8	n/a	n/a
1964	4.6	9.6	n/a	n/a
1965	4.1	8.1	n/a	n/a
1966	3.3	7.3	n/a	n/a
1967	3.4	7.4	n/a	n/a
1968	3.2	6.7	n/a	n/a
1969	3.1	6.4	n/a	n/a
1970	4.5	8.2	n/a	n/a
1971	5.4	9.9	n/a	n/a
1972	5.1	10.0	10.4	n/a
1973	4.3	9.0	9.4	7.5
1974	5.0	9.9	10.5	8.1
1975	7.8	13.8	14.8	12.2
1976	7.0	13.1	14.0	11.5
1977	6.2	13.1	14.0	10.1
1978	5.2	11.9	12.8	9.1
1979	5.1	11.3	12.3	8.3
1980	6.3	13.1	14.3	10.1
1981	6.7	14.2	15.6	10.4
1982	8.6	17.3	18.9	13.8
1983	8.4	17.8	19.5	13.7
1984	6.5	14.4	15.9	10.7
1985	6.2	13.7	15.1	10.5
1986	6.0	13.1	14.5	10.6
1987	5.3	11.6	13.0	8.8

n/a = not available.

Notes: 1948 is the first year unemployment rates by race were recorded. Black unemployment rates were first available in 1972 and Hispanic rates were first available in 1973.

Sources: For 1947 to 1970, U.S. Bureau of the Census, *Historical Statistics of the United States From Colonial Times to 1970,* Vol.1, Series D87-101, 1975; for 1971 to 1986, U.S. Department of Labor, Bureau of Labor Statistics, Federal Reserve Board Listing—Version 80.01/MDL, 1987; for 1987, U.S. Department of Labor, Bureau of Labor Statistics, 1988.

Youth Unemployment Rates by Race: 1972 to 1987

Youth unemployment rate is the percent of youths ages 16 to 19 who are seeking employment, including summer-time and part-time work.

Year	Total	White	Black	Hispanic
1972	16.2	14.2	35.4	n/a
1973	14.5	12.6	31.5	19.7
1974	16.0	14.0	35.0	19.8
1975	19.9	17.9	39.5	27.7
1976	19.0	16.9	39.3	23.8
1977	17.8	15.4	41.1	22.9
1978	16.4	13.9	38.7	20.7
1979	16.1	14.0	36.5	19.2
1980	17.8	15.5	38.5	22.5
1981	19.6	17.3	41.4	23.9
1982	23.2	20.4	48.0	29.9
1983	22.4	19.3	48.5	28.4
1984	18.9	16.0	42.7	24.1
1985	18.6	15.7	40.2	24.3
1986	18.3	15.6	39.3	24.7
1987	16.9	14.4	34.7	22.3

n/a = not available.

Sources: For 1972 to 1986, U.S. Department of Labor, Bureau of Labor Statistics, LABSTAT Database, April 1987; for 1987, U.S. Department of Labor, Bureau of Labor Statistics, 1988.

Unemployment Rates by State: 1986
(Annual Averages)

State	Number Unemployed	Rank by Number	Rate	Rank by Rate
Alabama	185,000	11	9.8	5
Alaska	28,000	42	10.8	4
Arizona	110,000	27	6.9	23
Arkansas	94,000	31	8.7	11
California	892,000	1	6.7	25
Colorado	126,000	23	7.4	20
Connecticut	66,000	34	3.8	48
Delaware	14,000	49	4.3	46
Florida	320,000	8	5.7	34
Georgia	178,000	15	5.9	33
Hawaii	24,000	43	4.8	42
Idaho	41,000	37	8.7	11
Illinois	461,000	4	8.1	16
Indiana	185,000	12	6.7	25
Iowa	100,000	29	7.0	21
Kansas	67,000	33	5.4	35
Kentucky	156,000	18	9.3	6
Louisiana	261,000	9	13.1	1
Maine	30,000	41	5.3	36
Maryland	105,000	28	4.5	45
Massachusetts	117,000	25	3.8	48
Michigan	385,000	7	8.8	10
Minnesota	118,000	24	5.3	36
Mississippi	136,000	21	11.7	3
Missouri	154,000	19	6.1	30
Montana	33,000	39	8.1	16
Nebraska	40,000	38	5.0	39
Nevada	32,000	40	6.0	31

Continued, next page

Unemployment Rates by State: 1986 (Cont.)
(Annual Averages)

State	Number Unemployed	Rank by Number	Rate	Rank by Rate
New Hampshire	16,000	47	2.8	50
New Jersey	196,000	10	5.0	39
New Mexico	62,000	35	9.2	7
New York	526,000	3	6.3	27
North Carolina	170,000	16	5.3	36
North Dakota	21,000	45	6.3	27
Ohio	426,000	5	8.1	16
Oklahoma	131,000	22	8.2	14
Oregon	114,000	26	8.5	13
Pennsylvania	386,000	6	6.8	24
Rhode Island	21,000	46	4.0	47
South Dakota	16,000	48	6.2	29
South Carolina	100,000	30	4.7	43
Tennessee	185,000	13	8.0	19
Texas	726,000	2	8.9	9
Utah	45,000	36	6.0	31
Vermont	14,000	50	4.7	43
Virginia	145,000	20	5.0	39
Washington	179,000	14	8.2	14
West Virginia	88,000	32	11.8	2
Wisconsin	169,000	17	7.0	21
Wyoming	22,000	44	9.0	8

Source: U.S. Department of Labor, Bureau of Labor Statistics, unpublished data, March 1987.

Chapter 9

Rich and Poor

Rich and Poor

While a rebounding economy during the 1980s helped improve the lives of millions of Americans, millions of others were losing ground. The income gap between rich and poor widened alarmingly in recent years as poverty overtook the lives of increasing numbers of children, older people and young families.

The Growing Income Gap

The gap between the poorest and the richest in this country in 1980 was the widest since the Census Bureau began gathering such data in 1947 (page 104). In 1986, families who were in the bottom 40% income bracket earned only 15% of the nation's total aggregate family income, while the top 40% earned almost 68% of the total.

In addition, the gap in individual incomes between the wealthiest and the poorest sections of the country has increased substantially since 1979, reversing a 50-year trend (pages 105–107). Growth in service and high-tech industries has boosted individual income levels in many New England, Mid-Atlantic and Western states, particularly Connecticut, New Jersey, Alaska and Massachusetts. On the other hand, a number of states in the Great Lakes, Plains, Rocky Mountains and Southwest which are economically dependent on agriculture, energy production and declining industries like coal and steel have experienced substantial reductions in individual income levels since 1979.

Rising Poverty

More than 32 million Americans were living in poverty in 1986, and another 11 million were living within 25% of the poverty line in 1986 (page 108). The statistic of "people below 125% of the poverty level" is often used to calculate the number of poor and near-poor people.

Three significant shifts in poverty patterns have taken place since 1959, the first year in which an official poverty measure was used:

• Between 1959 and 1973, the number of poor people fell from 39.5 million to just under 23 million, and the poverty rate was cut in half.

• From 1973 to 1978, poverty figures remained relatively stable.

• By 1983, however, the number of poor people had jumped to 35 million, the highest number since 1964. Today, the number still is 10 million greater than at its lowest point in 1973.

The percentage of all Americans living in poverty has ranged from a high of 22% in 1959 to a low of 11% in 1973 and back up to nearly 14% in 1986 (page 109). Although dramatic reductions in poverty rates have been achieved by blacks and older people in the past 25 years, poverty rates among blacks and Hispanics are still almost triple those of whites. A greater percentage of people living in the South, in rural areas and in central cities were living in poverty than those living elsewhere.

Child Poverty

Both the numbers and percentages of children living in poverty increased dramatically for all races in all areas of the country between 1979 and 1984, with the exception of those for southern black children, which remained stable—and high (page 110).

By 1984, almost 13 million children were poor, an increase of almost 30% in just six years. The percentage of American children living in poverty rose from 16% to 21%—a 31% increase. While 16% of white children were poor, almost 39% of Hispanic children and more than 46% of black children were living in poverty.

The greatest increase in both the numbers of poor children and in children's poverty rates between 1979 and 1984 occurred in the Midwest, where the numbers increased by 58% and the rate rose by 63%. The biggest gap between the poverty rates of black and white children also was found in the Midwest, where less than 16% of white children but more than 54% of black children lived in poverty.

Child poverty also rose by more than 41% in the West, which added 360,000 more poor children of Spanish origin between 1979 and 1984—a 71% increase. The South continued to have the greatest number of poor children in the country, although the group of children with the highest poverty *rates* shifted from black children in the South (44% in both 1979 and 1984) to children of Spanish origin in the Northeast (43% in 1979 to 55% in 1984).

For the growing number of children in female-headed homes, poverty has hit alarming levels (page 111). More than 45% of all children in families headed by women are poor, and more than 80% of children living in families headed by black females under the age of 25 live in poverty.

The Elderly Poor

Poverty among those age 65 and over has been reduced by two-thirds since 1959, from 35.2% to 12.4% of the total elderly population (page 112). Today, 3.5 million Americans age 65 and over are living in poverty. Elderly blacks and women are three times more likely than their white or male counterparts to be living in poverty.

Homelessness

An alarming increase in the number of homeless individuals and families during the past several years has generated national media coverage, task forces and new assistance programs. Unfortunately, the federal government does not collect data on homelessness, information without which it cannot anticipate or effectively respond to the problem. Private organizations, primarily advocacy groups, have attempted to fill the information gap.

Surveys by the National Coalition for the Homeless graphically illustrate the extent of this burgeoning national dilemma (page 113). In Los Angeles, for example, the number of homeless people is estimated between 70,000 and 90,000, yet the city reported only 5,000 beds in shelters for the homeless.

Another report, issued at the end of 1987 by the U.S. Conference of Mayors, recorded significant increases in requests for emergency shelter by individuals and families with children over the number of requests the year before (page 114). Kansas City and Philadelphia showed an increase in demand for emergency shelter of 40% or more, and in Charleston, the number of families with children requesting emergency shelter rose by 144% in one year's time. In nearly two-thirds of the cities evaluated in the report, homeless individuals and families were turned away from shelters.

Income Distribution of Families: 1947 to 1986

Year	Percent of Aggregate Income Earned By:		
	Bottom 40%	Middle 20%	Top 40%
1947*	16.8%	17.0%	66.3%
1950	16.4	17.4	66.2
1955	17.0	17.7	65.2
1960	17.0	17.8	65.3
1965	17.4	17.8	64.8
1970	17.6	17.6	64.7
1975	17.2	17.6	65.2
1980	16.7	17.5	65.9
1985	15.5	16.9	67.7
1986	15.4	16.8	67.7

*1947 was the first year income distribution data was collected.

Sources: For 1947 to 1970, U.S. Bureau of the Census, *Historical Statistics of the United States, from Colonial Times to 1970, Part 1,* Table G 31-138, 1975; for 1975, U.S. Bureau of the Census, "Money Income and Poverty Status of Families and Persons in the United States: 1974 and 1975 Revisions," *Current Population Reports,* Series P-60, No. 103, Table 5, 1976; for 1980, U.S. Bureau of the Census, "Money Income and Poverty Status of Families and Persons in the United States: 1980," *Current Population Reports,* Series P-60, No. 127, Table 5, 1981; for 1985, U.S. Bureau of the Census, "Money Income and Poverty Status of Families and Persons in the United States: 1985," *Current Population Reports,* Series P-60, No. 154, Table 4, 1986; for 1986, U.S. Bureau of the Census, "Money Income and Poverty Status of Families and Persons in the United States: 1986," *Current Population Reports,* Series P-60, No. 157, Table 4, 1987.

Per Capita Personal Income by State:
1979 and 1986
(Ranked by 1986 Income)

Per capita personal income is the income received by persons from all sources.

	1979 Income	1986 Income	1986 Rank	Percent of National Average: 1979	1986
Connecticut	$10,724	$19,600	1	119	134
New Jersey	10,277	18,626	2	114	127
Alaska	12,443	17,796	3	138	122
Massachusetts	9,444	17,722	4	105	121
New York	9,621	17,111	5	107	117
California	10,526	16,904	6	117	115
Maryland	9,672	16,864	7	107	115
New Hampshire	8,720	15,911	8	97	109
Illinois	10,090	15,586	9	112	106
Nevada	10,481	15,437	10	116	105
Virginia	8,710	15,408	11	96	105
Colorado	9,451	15,234	12	105	104
Delaware	9,181	15,010	13	102	103
Washington	9,841	15,009	14	109	103
Minnesota	9,226	14,994	15	102	102
Hawaii	9,506	14,886	16	105	102
Michigan	9,575	14,775	17	106	101
Kansas	9,290	14,650	18	103	100
Florida	8,719	14,646	19	97	100
Rhode Island	8,444	14,579	20	93	100
Pennsylvania	8,995	14,249	21	100	97
Ohio	8,958	13,933	22	99	95
Wisconsin	9,073	13,909	23	100	95
Missouri	8,615	13,789	24	95	94
Nebraska	8,853	13,742	25	98	94
Texas	8,834	13,478	26	98	92
Arizona	8,316	13,474	27	92	92

Continued, next page

Per Capita Personal Income by State:
1979 and 1986 (Cont.)

(Ranked by 1986 Income)

	1979 Income	1986 Income	1986 Rank	Percent of National Average:	
				1979	1986
Georgia	7,610	13,446	28	84	92
Iowa	9,091	13,348	29	101	91
Vermont	7,786	13,348	30	86	91
Oregon	9,174	13,328	31	102	91
Indiana	8,692	13,136	32	96	90
Maine	7,354	12,790	33	81	87
Wyoming	10,207	12,781	34	113	87
North Dakota	8,377	12,472	35	93	85
North Carolina	7,297	12,438	36	81	85
Oklahoma	8,371	12,283	37	93	84
Tennessee	7,389	12,002	38	82	82
South Dakota	8,062	11,814	39	89	81
Montana	8,146	11,803	40	90	81
New Mexico	7,463	11,422	41	83	78
Alabama	7,064	11,336	42	78	77
South Carolina	6,890	11,299	43	76	77
Kentucky	7,382	11,238	44	82	77
Idaho	7,814	11,223	45	87	77
Louisiana	7,668	11,193	46	85	76
Arkansas	6,945	11,073	47	77	76
Utah	7,408	10,981	48	82	75
West Virginia	7,220	10,576	49	80	72
Mississippi	6,441	9,716	50	71	66

Source: Bureau of Economic Analysis, *U.S. Department of Commerce News,*
BEA87-39, Table 2, August 20, 1987.

Per Capita Personal Income by Region:
1979 and 1986
(Ranked by 1986 Income)

Per capita personal income is the income received by persons from all sources.

Region	1979 Income	1986 Income	1986 Rank	Percent of National Average: 1979	1986
United States	**$9,033**	**$14,641**	–	100	100
New England	9,376	17,166	1	104	117
Mideast	9,584	16,565	2	106	113
Far West	10,321	16,348	3	114	112
Great Lakes	9,384	14,467	4	104	99
Plains	8,924	13,992	5	99	96
Southwest	8,617	13,195	6	95	90
Rocky Mountain	8,658	13,146	7	96	90
Southeast	7,676	12,694	8	85	87

Note: New England includes CT, ME, MA, NH, RI and VT; Mideast includes DE, MD, NJ, NY and PA; Far West includes CA, NV, OR, WA, AK and HI; Great Lakes includes IL, IN, MI, OH and WI; Plains includes IA, KS, MN, MO, NE, ND and SD; Southwest includes AZ, NM, OK AND TX; Rocky Mountains includes CO, ID, MT, UT and WY; Southeast includes AL, AR, FL GA, KY, LA, MS, NC, SC, TN, VA and WV.

Source: Bureau of Economic Analysis, *U.S. Department of Commerce News*, BEA87-39, Table 2, August 20, 1987.

People Living in Poverty: 1959 to 1986

The **poverty level** was determined by the Social Security Administration in 1964 to be three times the cost of obtaining a minimally adequate diet. In 1986, the poverty level cut-off for an individual was $5,572 and $11,203 for a family of four. The poverty level is based solely on money income, and does not include noncash benefits such as Medicaid, food stamps, and public housing.

People living below 125% of the poverty level is often used to estimate the number of poor and near poor in society.

Year	People Below Poverty Level Number (in thousands)	Percent	People Below 125% of Poverty Level Number (in thousands)	Percent
1959	39,490	22.4	54,942	31.1
1960	39,851	22.2	54,560	30.4
1961	39,628	21.9	54,280	30.0
1962	38,625	21.0	53,119	28.8
1963	36,436	19.5	50,778	27.1
1964	36,055	19.0	49,819	26.3
1965	33,185	17.3	46,163	24.1
1966	28,510	14.7	41,267	21.3
1967	27,769	14.2	39,206	20.0
1968	25,389	12.8	35,905	18.2
1969	24,147	12.1	34,665	17.4
1970	25,420	12.6	35,624	17.6
1971	25,559	12.5	36,501	17.8
1972	24,460	11.9	34,653	16.8
1973	22,973	11.1	32,828	15.8
1974	23,370	11.2	33,666	16.1
1975	25,877	12.3	37,182	17.6
1976	24,975	11.8	35,509	16.7
1977	24,720	11.6	35,659	16.7
1978	24,497	11.4	34,155	15.8
1979	26,072	11.7	36,616	16.4
1980	29,272	13.0	40,658	18.1
1981	31,822	14.0	43,748	19.3
1982	34,398	15.0	46,520	20.3
1983	35,303	15.2	47,150	20.3
1984	33,700	14.4	45,288	19.4
1985	33,064	14.0	44,166	18.7
1986	32,370	13.6	43,486	18.2

Sources: For 1959 to 1986 "Poverty Level" and 1981 to 1986 "125% of Poverty Level," U.S. Bureau of the Census, "Money Income and Poverty Status of Families and Persons in the United States: 1986," *Current Population Reports (CPR)* Series P-60, No. 157, Table 16 and 17, 1987; for 1959 to 1976 "125% of Poverty Level," U.S. Bureau of the Census, *CPR*, Series P-60, No. 115, "Characteristics of the Population Below Poverty Level: 1976," Table 2, 1978; for 1977 to 1980 "125% of Poverty Level," U.S. Bureau of the Census, *CPR*, Series P-60, No. 152, "Characteristics of the Population Below Poverty Level: 1984," Table 2, 1986.

Percent of People Living in Poverty by Region, Age, Race, Sex and Family Status: 1959 to 1986

Characteristic	1959	1973	1986
United States	**22.4%**	**11.1%**	**13.6%**
South	35.4	15.3	16.1
Northeast	*	*	10.5
Midwest*	16.0	9.1	13.0
West	*	*	13.2
Non-Metropolitan Areas	33.2	14.0	18.1
Metropolitan Areas	15.3	9.7	12.3
Central Cities	18.3	14.0	18.0
Suburbs	12.2	6.4	8.4
Under 18 years	26.9	14.2	19.8
18–64	17.4	8.4	10.9
65 and over	35.2	16.3	12.4
White	18.1	8.4	11.0
Black	55.1	31.4	31.1
Spanish Origin	n/a	n/a	27.3
Male	n/a	n/a	17.5
Female	n/a	n/a	25.1
Living in families	20.8	9.7	10.9
Male-headed**	18.2	6.0	11.4
Female-headed**	49.4	37.5	34.6
Unrelated	46.1	25.6	21.6

n/a = not available.

*1959 and 1973 data includes Northeast, Midwest, and West combined.

**For 1986, male-headed signifies no wife present and female-headed signifies no husband present. For other years, spouses need not be absent to be male- or female-headed households.

Notes: 1959 was the first year the U.S. Bureau of the Census collected poverty data. In 1973, the U.S. Bureau of the Census recorded the lowest poverty rates ever in the United States.

Sources: For 1959, William P. O'Hare, "Poverty in America: Trends and New Patterns," *Population Bulletin,* Population Reference Bureau, Tables 2 and 4, 1985; for 1973, U.S. Bureau of the Census, "Characteristics of the Low-Income Population: 1973," *Current Population Reports,* Series P-60, No. 98, Tables 3 and 8, 1975; for 1986, U.S. Bureau of the Census, "Money Income and Poverty Status of Families and Persons in the United States: 1986," *Current Population Reports,* Series P-60, No. 157, Tables B and 18, 1987.

Children Under 18 Living in Poverty by Race and Spanish Origin: 1979 and 1984

(Numbers in thousands)

Region, Race & Spanish Origin	----- 1979 -----		----- 1984 -----	
	Number	Rate (Percent)	Number	Rate (Percent)
United States	**9,994**	**16.0**	**12,929**	**21.0**
White	5,909	11.4	8,086	16.1
Black	3,746	40.8	4,320	46.2
Spanish Origin*	1,504	27.7	2,317	38.7
Northeast	**2,013**	**15.4**	**2,486**	**20.5**
White	1,369	12.3	1,675	16.4⁻
Black	611	36.0	764	45.7
Spanish Origin*	418	43.4	588	55.0
Midwest	**2,088**	**12.6**	**3,291**	**20.5**
White	1,291	9.0	2,196	15.8
Black	754	40.2	1,029	54.2
Spanish Origin*	100	20.4	228	39.0
South	**4,319**	**20.3**	**4,789**	**22.9**
White	2,083	13.0	2,476	15.9
Black	2,168	44.3	2,233	44.4
Spanish Origin*	477	29.0	632	34.2
West	**1,574**	**13.3**	**2,363**	**18.8**
White	1,166	11.5	1,739	16.4
Black	213	30.3	294	38.9
Spanish Origin*	509	21.8	869	35.0

*A small part of the increase in the number of poor children of Spanish origin is attributable to changes in estimating procedures instituted by the Census Bureau in 1984.

Sources: U.S. Bureau of the Census, as cited by the Select Committee on Children, Youth, and Families, U.S. House of Representatives, 99th Congress *Safety Net Programs: Are They Reaching Poor Children?,* Table I-1, September 1986.

Percent of Families with Children Living In Poverty: 1984

Family Type and Ages of Head	– – – Percent in Poverty – – –		
	Total	White	Black
Female-Headed Families	45.7	38.8	58.4
Head under age 25	76.8	72.1	82.8
Head age 25 to 44	43.8	37.5	56.5
Two-Parent Families	9.4	8.5	16.6
Head under age 25	21.8	20.8	33.2
Head age 25 to 44	8.4	7.7	14.9

Note: Data for Hispanic families are not published.

Source: U.S. Bureau of the Census, "Characteristics of the Population Below the Poverty Level: 1984," *Current Population Reports*, Series P-60, No. 152, Table 15, 1986 as cited by the Children's Defense Fund *Children's Defense Budget*, 1987.

Elderly Living in Poverty: 1959 to 1986
(Numbers in thousands)

	1959	1970	1980	1986
Total, Ages 65 and over*	**15,571**	**19,484**	**24,656**	**28,040**
Total in Poverty	5,481	4,793	3,711	3,477
Percent in Poverty	35.2%	24.6%	15.7%	12.4%
Poverty by Race:				
White	33.1%	22.6%	13.6%	10.7%
Black	62.5%	48.0%	38.1%	31.0%
Poverty by Sex of Family Head:				
Female	49.2%	41.1%	27.8%	23.1%
Male	30.2%	16.7%	9.5%	7.1%
Percent with Income Below 125% of Poverty Level	n/a	33.5%	25.7%	20.5%

n/a = not available.

*Population data differs from previous charts due to poverty surveys ending at a different time of year than population surveys.

Source: For 1959 to 1980, U.S. Bureau of the Census, "Money Income and Poverty Status of Families and Persons in the United States: 1985," *Current Population Reports*, Series P-60, No. 154, 1986 as cited by The Urban Institute *Toward Ending Poverty Among the Elderly and Disabled: Policy Financing Options*, 1987; for 1986, U.S. Bureau of the Census, "Money Income and Poverty Status of Families and Persons in the United States: 1986," *Current Population Reports*, Series P-60, No. 157, Tables 16 and 17, 1987.

Homeless People in 29 Cities: 1986 and 1987*

City	Estimated Number of Homeless	Available Number of Beds	Percent Increase in Homeless Over Previous Year
Albuquerque	1,300-5,000	350	30
Atlanta	6,000-10,000	3,000	25
Boston	5,000-7,000	2,351	30
Burlington, VT*	75-120	60	10
Charleston, WV*	300	200	50
Chicago	25,000-30,000	2,800	25
Cincinnati*	1,600	800	n/a
Cleveland	5,000-20,000	500	10-15
Dallas	4,000-14,000	1,724	20
Denver	3,000	950	15-20
Des Moines	1,000-1,500	529	10
Laramie, WY	150-200	n/a	100
Los Angeles	50,000	5,000	25
Manchester, NH	1,200	70	10
Miami	10,000	409	25
Milwaukee	6,500	650	30
Minneapolis	23,500	1,100	31
Nashville	825**	765	8
New Haven, CT	3,200	344	15-20
New Orleans	1,200-5,000	577	20
New York	70,000-90,000	30,000	15
Phoenix	6,500	800-1,000	30
Portland, OR	4,000	2,301	10
Providence, RI*	3,500	177	25
Richmond, VA	2,000-6,000	200-290	30
Seattle	3,500-5,000	1,200-14,000	30
St. Louis*	10,000-15,000	428	100
Tucson*	2,000-3,000	165	25
Washington, DC	10,000-15,000	2,500	25-30

n/a = not available.

*Data for Burlington, Charleston, Cincinnati, Providence, St. Louis and Tucson apply to 1986, all other data is for 1987.

**This includes only those people sleeping in the downtown area and in shelters on June 19, 1987.

Sources: National Coalition for the Homeless, *Pushed Out: America's Homeless,* November 1987; for 1986 data: National Coalition for the Homeless, *National Neglect/National Shame, America's Homeless: Outlook, Winter 1986–1987,* September 1986.

Homelessness Rates in Major Cities:
1987

City	Percent Increase In Demand for Emergency Shelter	Percent Increase In Families With Children	Are People Turned Away From Shelters?
Boston	10	10	No
Charleston	23	144	Yes
Chicago	7	n/a	Yes
Cleveland	10	20	Yes
Detroit	15	15	No
Kansas City	44	3	Yes
Los Angeles	25	40	Yes
Louisville	0	0	n/a
Minneapolis	20	n/a	No
Nashville	23	n/a	Yes
New Orleans	20	n/a	Yes
New York City	16	18	No
Norfolk	17	30	Yes
Philadelphia	40	66	No
Phoenix	15	10	Yes
Portland, OR	12	15	Yes
Portsmouth, VA	n/a	n/a	Yes
Providence	30	75	Yes
Saint Paul	8	2	No
Salt Lake City	20	20	No
San Antonio	7	20	No
San Francisco	25	n/a	Yes
Seattle	25	n/a	Yes
Trenton	15	15	Yes
Washington, DC	30	40	No

n/a = not available.

Source: The U.S. Conference of Mayors, *The Continuing Growth of Hunger, Homelessness and Poverty: 1987,* December 1987.

Chapter 10

Water Use and Abuse

Water Use and Abuse

Overpopulation and contamination seriously threaten the precious little fresh water that exists. The earth's population size has created intense competition for an ever-dwindling per-capita supply of fresh water. And industry, energy production and agriculture generate millions of gallons of water pollutants daily, endangering our nation's environment and health.

Population Growth and Declining Water Levels

Though life is impossible without fresh water, it is in shockingly finite supply. The World Resources Institute calculates that 97% of the Earth's water is saline, and of the 3% that is fresh, an estimated 77% is frozen in glaciers and ice caps. Groundwater and soil moisture make up much of the fresh water that remains, leaving only 0.35% in lakes and swamps and an infinitesimal 0.01% in rivers and streams.

But while these proportions have remained roughly the same for a hundred centuries or more, the Earth's population has exploded.

Between 1950 and 1980, the U.S. population increased by more than 50%, from 150 million to 230 million, while the withdrawal of water from the nation's streams, reservoirs, lakes and underground aquifers increased by 150%, from 180 billion to 450 billion gallons per day (page 120).

The practice of groundwater mining, the depletion of an aquifer at a rate that exceeds its replenishment, is an increasingly serious problem (page 121). When such "overdrafts" occur, the damage to an aquifer is irreversible. Drawn-down aquifers near coastal river systems are infiltrated by salt water, contaminating the water. In others, the land surface sinks into the aquifer to fill the space left by pumped-out water, permanently preventing replenishment of the aquifer.

In many fast-growing southwestern states, there is barely enough precipitation to sustain vegetation cover, much less enough to meet the voluminous demands of humans. In the Colorado River Basin, for example, yearly water consumption already exceeds renewable supplies by 5%, generating a water deficit. Salt-water intrusion is contaminating the river and irrigated farm land, and water tables have dropped precipitously in fast-growing cities like Phoenix. As former Governor Richard Lamm of Colorado notes, "We talk scarcity, yet we have set our largest cities in the deserts, and then have insisted on surrounding ourselves with Kentucky bluegrass. Our words are those of the Sahara Desert; our policies are those of the Amazon River."

Groundwater Pollution

Not coincidentally, many areas of the country vulnerable to groundwater *depletion* are also experiencing groundwater *pollution* (page 122). Sources of such pollution include natural trace elements, hazardous waste sites, septic tanks, leaking underground sewer lines and oil storage tanks, runoff from farms, streets, highways and mines, and industrial and municipal wastes. Nitrates from fertilizers, household and industrial chemicals, fossil fuels and hazardous wastes are contaminating wells and aquifers in every part of the country.

As part of its National Pesticide Survey, the EPA assessed the vulnerability of all 3,144 U.S. counties to well-water contamination by agricultural pesticides (page 123). As expected, the counties judged most vulnerable were located in Florida and other fast-growing areas of the southeastern and Atlantic coastal plains where groundwater levels are perilously close to the surface. Those least vulnerable were generally located in the West, where groundwater levels are deep enough to offer some protection against pesticide contamination.

Surface Water Contamination

Surface water – the water in streams, lakes and reservoirs, as opposed to wells and aquifers – is most often contaminated by industrial and municipal discharges of untreated or inadequately treated waste water, as well as by the pesticides, fertilizers, bacteria, salts, toxic metals and other pollutants which wash from farms, mines, highways and city streets into nearby bodies of water.

In a state-by-state report of river and lake contamination, seven states reported pollution by seven or more contaminants in 1984 (pages 124–127). Of these, five are located in the fast-growing Sunbelt, and all but one are states which are either already densely populated or are experiencing rapid population growth.

Nutrient Loading

"Nutrient loading" is another form of surface water pollution. When nitrate and phosphorus are added to rivers from drain pipes, sewage treatment plants, urban and agricultural runoff, they act as plant nutrients, often generating excessive vegetation. As this vegetation decomposes, it can seriously deplete oxygen levels in the water, as well as giving it an unpleasant odor, appearance and taste.

An assessment of nutrient delivery to the drainage basins of the nation's rivers between 1974 and 1981 found widespread increases in nitrate in Atlantic Coast estuaries, the Gulf of Mexico and the Great Lakes (page 127). These increases reflect a 68% increase in the application of nitrogen fertilizers during the 1970s, as well as dense livestock populations and acid rain containing high concentrations of nitrogen oxides from industrial sources.

Phosphorus loads to coastal areas either changed only slightly between 1974 and 1981 or declined in response to regulations restricting their use. In Gulf Coast and Pacific Northwest estuaries, however, phosphorus loads increased. The increase of phosphorus is associated with various measures of agricultural land use, including fertilized acreage and cattle population density.

Contamination of Marine Waters

Many of the nation's estuaries—the breeding grounds of most marine life—are already seriously polluted. The open ocean remains relatively uncontaminated thus far, although the Office of Technology Assessment (OTA) points out that hundreds of millions of gallons of municipal sewage effluent are dumped into marine waters every day by treatment plants in coastal states (page 128).

The OTA study notes that while only 3.5% of the approximately 15,500 publicly owned sewage treatment plants in the U.S. discharged effluent directly into estuaries and coastal waters in 1982, these tended to be large facilities which serve densely populated coastal areas and generate 25% of the nation's municipal waste water. More than 60% of total discharges occurred in the North Atlantic, where the worst offender was New York, the nation's second most populous state. California, the most populous state, generated 20% of the nation's total effluent discharge into marine waters.

According to the U.S. Census Bureau, the number of people living in coastal counties mushroomed by more than 80% between 1950 and 1984. More than 50% of the population lived within 50 miles of a marine coastline in 1984. As coastal populations continue to grow, they will generate increasing pressures on municipal sewage treatment plants to continue marine dumping.

Water* Withdrawal and Population Trends: 1950 to 1980

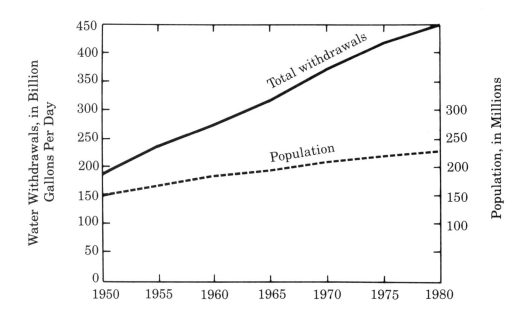

*Surface water and groundwater.

Source: U.S. Geological Society, *National Water Summary 1983; Hydrologic Events and Issues,* Water-Supply Paper 2250, Figure 11, 1984.

Declining Groundwater Levels and Related Problems: 1983

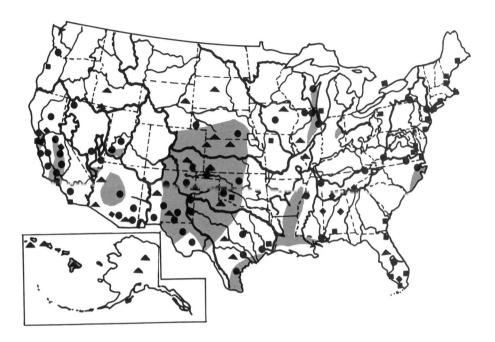

Area Problem

� Area in which significant groundwater overdraft is occurring

☐ Unshaded area may not be problem-free, but the problem was not considered major

Boundaries

━━ Water resources region

── Subregion

Specific Problems (as identified by federal and state/regional study teams)

● Declining groundwater levels

▲ Diminished springflow and streamflow

◆ Formation of fissures and subsidence*

■ Salt-water intrusion into freshwater aquifers**

*__Subsidence__ is the collapse of soils above aquifers due to removal of large quantities of underground water. This compaction is irreversible; the sediments are altered permanently and water cannot return to the storage area.

**__Salt-water intrusion__ is the displacement of groundwater by advancing salt water. This often occurs when groundwater declines below sea level.

Source: V.J. Pye et al., *Groundwater Contamination in the United States,* (Philadelphia: University of Pennsylvania Press), 1983 as cited by World Resources Institute and International Institute for Environment and Development, *World Resources 1986; An Assessment of the Resource Base that Supports the Global Economy,* Figure 8.10, 1986.

Groundwater Pollution: 1983

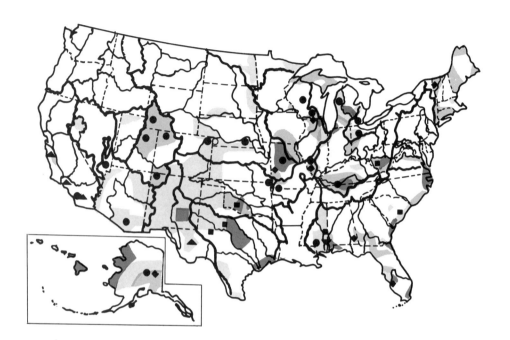

Area Problems

▨ Significant groundwater pollution is occurring

▨ Salt-water intrusion* or groundwater is naturally salty

▨ High level of minerals or other dissolved solids in groundwater

☐ Unshaded area may not be problem-free, but problem was not considered major

Specific Sources of Pollution

▼ Municipal and industrial wastes including wastes from oil and gas fields

● Toxic industrial wastes

◆ Landfill leachate

▲ Irrigation return waters

■ Wastes from well drilling, harbor dredging, and excavation for drainage systems

○ Well injection of industrial waste liquids

*Salt-water intrusion** is the displacement of groundwater by advancing salt water. This often occurs when groundwater declines below sea level.

Source: V.J. Pye et al., *Groundwater Contamination in the United States,* (Philadelphia: University of Pennsylvania Press), 1983 as cited by World Resources Institute and International Institute for Environment and Development, *World Resources 1986; An Assessment of the Resource Base that Supports the Global Economy,* Figure 8.12, 1986.

Counties' Vulnerability to Groundwater Pollution*:
1987

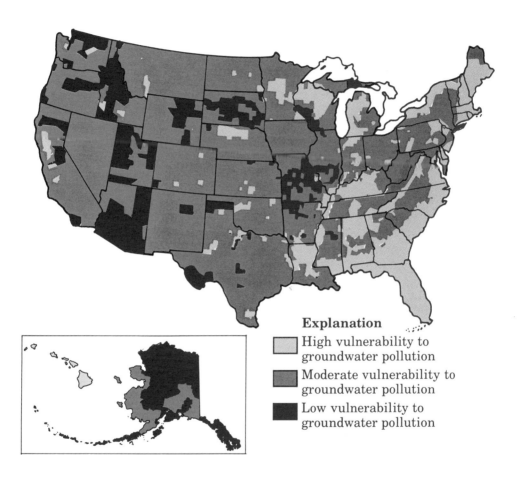

Explanation

High vulnerability to groundwater pollution

Moderate vulnerability to groundwater pollution

Low vulnerability to groundwater pollution

*Assessed solely on the hydrogeologic characteristics of groundwater regions and does not take into account the presence of pollutants in the environment.

Note: Variations within a county can be great, allowing localized, highly vulnerable areas within some counties to be overshadowed by the prominence of surrounding lower vulnerability areas. Such averaging is necessary to help focus on the more highly vulnerable counties.

Source: Office of Pesticide Programs, U.S. Environmental Protection Agency, *Groundwater Vulnerability Assessment of the National Pesticide Survey*, 1987.

River and Lake Contaminants by State:* 1984

STATE	Bacteria	Excess Nutrients	BOD/ Low Oxygen	Turbidity/ TSS	Dissolved Solids	Metals Problem	Other Toxics	pH Problem	Ammonia
Alabama		x	x		x			x	
Alaska				x					
Arizona	x	x	x	x	x	x	x	x	
Arkansas	x	x	x	x	x	x			
California	x	x	x		x	x	x	x	
Colorado	x					x			x
Connecticut	x	x	x			x	x		x
Delaware	x	x	x				x		
Florida	x	x	x	x		x	x	x	
Georgia	x	x	x				x	x	
Hawaii	x	x		x					
Idaho	x	x		x		x			
Illinois	x	x	x	x	x			x	x
Iowa	x	x	x	x					x
Kansas	x		x		x	x			
Kentucky	x	x		x		x	x		
Louisiana	x		x				x		
Maine	x		x				x		
Maryland	x	x	x	x			x	x	
Massachusetts	x	x	x				x		
Michigan		x	x	x		x	x		
Minnesota	x	x		x			x		
Mississippi	x	x	x	x			x		
Missouri	x			x		x	x	x	
Montana				x	x	x		x	
Nebraska	x			x					
New Hampshire	x	x	x						
New Jersey	x	x	x	x			x	x	

Continued, next page

River and Lake Contaminants by State:* 1984 (Cont.)

STATE	Bacteria	Excess Nutrients	BOD/ Low Oxygen	Turbidity/ TSS	Dissolved Solids	Metals Problem	Other Toxics	pH Problem	Ammonia
New Mexico	x	x	x						x
New York	x	x	x	x		x	x	x	
North Carolina	x	x	x	x		x		x	x
North Dakota		x		x	x				
Ohio	x		x			x	x		x
Oklahoma	x		x			x		x	
Oregon	x	x							
Pennsylvania		x	x	x		x		x	x
Rhode Island	x		x	x			x		
South Carolina	x	x	x				x	x	
South Dakota	x	x		x		x		x	x
Tennessee	x			x	x	x		x	x
Texas	x	x	x		x	x	x	x	
Utah		x		x	x				x
Vermont	x	x	x			x		x	
Virginia	x	x	x				x		
Washington	x	x	x	x			x	x	
Wisconsin	x	x	x	x			x		x
Wyoming	x	x		x	x	x			

*See next page for definitions of water pollutants.

Note: Indiana, Nevada and West Virginia are omitted from this table. They did not file reports in time for inclusion in the study.

Source: U.S. Environmental Protection Agency, *National Water Quality Inventory, 1984 Report to Congress,* EPA 440/4-85-029, Figures 2-2 to 2-10, 1985.

Definitions of Water Pollutants

Bacteria: Fecal coliform bacteria are indicators of the possible presence of harmful disease-causing organisms that make waters unsafe for human recreational contact and that can make shellfish unsafe for human consumption. Bacteria are widely used as a measure of "swimmability." Possible sources of bacteria include municipal wastewater treatment plants, combined sewers (storm and sanitary sewers combined), urban runoff, feedlots, pastures and rangeland, septic systems and natural sources.

Nutrients: Nutrients are substances such as nitrogen and phosphorus that support and stimulate aquatic plant growth. In excess, nutrients over-stimulate weed and plant growth, causing unpleasant tastes, odors and reduced oxygen levels. Nutrients originate from municipal wastewater treatment plants, septic systems, combined sewers, and runoff from construction sites, urban lawns and agricultural land.

Biochemical Oxygen Demand (BOD)/Low Oxygen: Aquatic organisms such as fish and water-dwelling insects require minimum levels of dissolved oxygen if they are to survive. Biochemical oxygen demand (BOD) is the term applied to organic loads that reduce dissolved oxygen levels. Possible sources of BOD and low oxygen levels include municipal wastewater treatment plants, industries (particularly pulp and paper mills), combined sewers and natural sources.

Turbidity/Total Suspended Solids (TSS): Suspended solids such as soil sediment cause turbidity and can harm aquatic life. The suspended solids can carry nutrients, pesticides, and bacteria which are also harmful. Turbidity is caused by erosion of agricultural areas, construction sites and forestlands as well as the natural erosion of watersheds.

Total Dissolved Solids and Salts: Total dissolved solids include inorganic salts, small amounts of dissolved organic matter and other dissolved materials in water. Salinity problems are often naturally occurring in the West, and are aggravated by low flows and heavy use and reuse of water for irrigation and other agricultural purposes. Excess dissolved solids are also objectionable in drinking water; they can affect the health of people on low sodium diets, cause unpleasant mineral tastes, and increase the chances of plumbing system corrosion. Sources of total dissolved solids include agriculture, mining, urban runoff, and combined sewers.

Metals and Toxics: Heavy metals such as arsenic, cadmium, lead and mercury and other industrial toxics such as cyanide, phenols, PCBs, pesticides and dioxins can cause significant short-term and long-term damage to aquatic and human life and are potentially lethal to both. Heavy metals and toxic organic chemicals are increasingly an environmental concern but little monitoring data is currently available. Sources include industries, municipal wastewater treatment plants, agriculture, land disposal sites, urban runoff and combined sewers.

pH: Alkaline or acidic substances can change the natural pH of a waterbody, often causing extensive and severe water degradation and impairing most forms of aquatic life. Acids can leach metals such as aluminum, mercury and zinc from soil and sediments, resulting in toxic conditions for aquatic life. Changes in pH are most often caused by atmospheric deposition and mine drainage.

Ammonia: Sources of ammonia most often are municipal wastewater treatment plants and combined sewers. If present in high concentrations, ammonia is toxic to aquatic life.

Sources: U.S. Environmental Protection Agency, *National Water Quality Inventory, 1984 Report to Congress,* EPA-440/4-85-029, 1985; and The Conservation Foundation, *State of the Environment; An Assessment at Mid-Decade,* 1984.

Nutrient Loading of Rivers in Coastal Areas: 1974 to 1981

Nutrient loading here is defined as the total amount of nitrate and phosphorus added to surface waters via rivers. The pollutants originate upstream from drainage pipes, sewage management facilities and urban and agricultural runoff. Phosphorus and nitrates act as plant nutrients which, when present in unnaturally large amounts, can result in excess weed and plant growth, causing unpleasant tastes, odors, and reduced oxygen levels.

Region	Percent Change in Load 1974 to 1981	
	Total Nitrate	Total Phosphorus
Northeast Atlantic Coast	32	-20
Long Island Sound/NY Bight	26	-1
Chesapeake Bay	29	-0.5
Southeast Atlantic Coast	20	12
Albemarle/Pamlico Sound	28	0
Gulf Coast	46	55
Great Lakes	36	-7
Pacific Northwest	6	34
California	-5	-5

Source: R.A. Smith, R.B. Alexander, M.G. Wolman, "Water Quality Trends in the Nation's Rivers," *Science,* Vol. 235, No. 4796, Table 3, March 27, 1987.

Effluent Discharges from
Municipal Sewage Treatment Plants
Directly into Marine Waters, by State: 1982

Effluent is sewage water after treatment. It contains a lower concentration of pollutants than raw sewage.

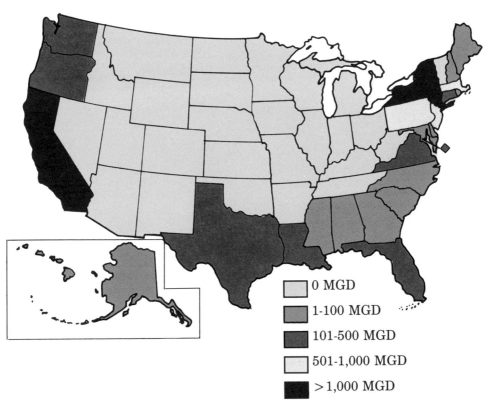

Legend:
- 0 MGD
- 1-100 MGD
- 101-500 MGD
- 501-1,000 MGD
- > 1,000 MGD

MGD = million gallons per day

Amount of Effluent Discharged into Marine Waters (In million gallons per day)	
United States:	**6,645**
Northern Atlantic Region:	4,150
Southern Atlantic Region:	380
Gulf of Mexico Region:	522
California and Hawaii:	1,282
Northern Pacific Region:	383

Source: Office of Technology Assessment and Science Applications International Corporation, as cited by the Office of Technology Assessment, *Wastes in Marine Environments*, Figure 4, 1987.

Chapter 11

**Airborne Poisons:
First the Good News, Then . . .**

National Air Pollution Emission Levels
Acid Precipitation and Deposition

Airborne Poisons: First the Good News, Then . . .

Substantial progress has been made in controlling air pollution since passage of the Clean Air Act in 1970. However, millions of people still breathe air that is unhealthy, up to $4.5 billion worth of crops are lost annually to airborne pollutants and acid deposition is killing growing numbers of our nation's forests and lakes.

National Air Pollution Emission Levels

The Environmental Protection Agency (EPA) recently warned 42 governors that their states were not meeting air pollution standards, and the National Clean Air Coalition reports that 100 million Americans "live in places where the air is so polluted that breathing is hazardous to our health."

Chronic exposure to air pollutants such as suspended particulates, nitrogen oxides, carbon monoxide and lead can aggravate respiratory illnesses and cause anemia, convulsions, kidney and brain damage and even death. Other pollutants are equally destructive, in different ways. Volatile organic compounds, for example, combine with other chemicals to form a type of ozone which damages crops and human tissues.

While levels of some air pollutants increased after passage of the Clean Air Act, significant progress was made in the decade from 1976 to 1985 in several of the six pollutants measured by EPA (pages 133–134). Lead levels, for example, fell by 86%, largely because of reductions in the lead content of gasoline. Levels of suspended particulates fell by 25%, and both carbon monoxide and sulfur oxide levels declined 21% during the decade.

In the summer of 1987, EPA released 1984-86 data on ozone and carbon monoxide levels in major metropolitan areas. Sixty-two areas, mostly major cities, failed to meet ozone standards. While the agency reported improved ozone levels in 16 metropolitan areas, it noted that weather conditions, rather than real pollution reductions, were responsible for much of the change. For carbon monoxide, EPA reported that 65 areas, also mostly major cities, failed to meet standards. While 23 areas showed enough improvement to meet standards, 7 others were added to the list of violators, for a net improvement of 16.

Acid Precipitation and Deposition

Air pollution is no longer viewed as a local problem; it is now clear that a number of airborne pollutants regularly cross state and national boundaries to poison crops, forests and lakes in an ever-expanding geographic range.

Acid, contained in precipitation and deposits not carried by moisture, is a major long-range airborne pollutant. The problem is created when sulfates and nitrates generated from power plants, industries and motor vehicles combine with atmospheric moisture to form sulfuric and nitric acids, which then fall to earth in rain, snow, fog or as dry deposits. Acid precipitation and deposits damage lungs, manmade structures, crops, forests, lakes, streams and aquatic wildlife. Although the causes and effects of acid precipitation and deposition have been known for some time, the official U.S. government response has been limited.

Acid deposition in the northeastern United States has increased by almost 16 times in some areas in the past 30 years (page 135–137). The parts of the country most severely affected are in the Appalachian Mountains from Georgia to New England. In Kentucky, for instance, a 1986 study by the U.S. Forest Service found that 77% of all the Eastern white pine stands surveyed showed air pollution damage. Most lakes in New York State's Adirondack mountains are so dangerously acidic that little can live in them. Precipitation in many areas can be as acidic as vinegar (pH3) or worse: one fog in Connecticut was measured with a pH of 2.2, the acid concentration of bottled lemon juice, and a rainstorm that pelted Wheeling, W.Va. had a pH of 1.5 (battery acid is pH1).

Other areas of the country are affected as well. For example, more than half the lakes sampled by the EPA in the relatively unpopulated western mountain states of Idaho, Montana, Oregon, Washington, Wyoming and Utah were endangered by acidification in 1986 (page 138).

Annual Emissions of Air Pollutants:*
1940 to 1985
(Millions of metric tons per year)

Year	Suspended Particulate Matter	Sulfur Oxides	Nitrogen Oxides	Volatile Organics	Carbon Monoxide	Lead**
1940	22.8	18.0	6.8	18.5	81.6	n/a
1950	24.5	20.3	9.3	20.8	86.3	n/a
1960	21.1	20.0	12.8	23.6	88.4	n/a
1970	18.1	28.2	18.1	27.1	98.8	203.8
1971	16.7	26.8	18.6	26.5	96.8	220.8
1972	15.2	27.4	19.7	26.5	94.4	231.7
1973	14.1	28.7	20.2	25.8	90.0	202.7
1974	12.4	27.0	19.7	24.2	85.1	162.1
1975	10.4	25.6	19.2	22.8	81.2	147.0
1976	9.7	26.2	20.3	24.0	85.9	153.1
1977	9.1	26.3	21.0	23.9	81.9	141.2
1978	9.2	24.5	21.0	24.5	81.5	127.9
1979	9.0	24.5	21.1	23.9	78.4	108.7
1980	8.5	23.2	20.4	22.7	76.2	70.6
1981	7.9	22.3	20.5	21.4	73.5	55.9
1982	7.0	21.3	19.7	19.9	67.4	54.4
1983	6.7	20.6	19.1	20.5	70.4	46.3
1984	7.0	21.4	19.7	21.5	69.9	40.1
1985	7.3	20.7	20.0	21.3	67.5	21.0

n/a = not available.

 *See next page for definitions of air pollutants.
**Lead is measured in thousands of metric tons per year.

Sources: For 1940 to 1984, U.S. Environmental Protection Agency, *National Air Pollutant Emission Estimates,* 1980-1984, EPA-450/4-85-014, 1986; *National Air Qualtiy and Emissions Trends Report, 1985,* EPA-450/4-87-001, 1987.

Definitions of Air Pollutants

Suspended particulate matter—minute dust particles—results primarily from industrial processes and fuel combustion. Smaller particulates can carry toxic substances, be toxic themselves, and can imbed themselves in lung tissue. Suspended particulate matter can aggravate respiratory illnesses.

Sulfur oxides largely originate from the combustion of coal and oil by electrical utilities and industrial processes. Sulfur dioxide is a main contributor, along with nitrogen oxides, to acid deposition.

Nitrogen oxides are caused by the combustion of fuel by industry, automobiles and electrical utilities. Nitrogen oxides contribute to photochemical smog and ozone, which corrode wood and stone and threaten the health of humans and animals. Nitrogen oxides aggravate respiratory illnesses and combine with water in the atmosphere to form acid deposition.

Volatile organic compounds originate from the combustion of fossil fuels by automobiles and power stations, industrial processes, refineries, and volatilization of organic solvents and fuels. In the presence of sunlight, these organic compounds contribute to the formation of ozone. Ozone damages plant and animal tissue, prematurely ages the lungs and causes other respiratory damage.

Carbon monoxide is formed from combustion of fossil fuels, mostly gasoline and diesel fuel. Exposure to carbon monoxide is greatest in urban areas. If present at high concentrations, carbon monoxide can cause drowsiness, slowed reflexes and possibly death.

Lead in the atmosphere results mainly from the combustion of lead-containing gasoline by automobiles. Chronic exposure to lead, a heavy metal, can lead to anemia, convulsions, and kidney and brain damage.

Sources: The Conservation Foundation, *State of the Environment; An Assessment at Mid-Decade,* 1984; and World Resources Institute and International Institute for Environment and Development, *World Resources 1987; An Assessment of the Resource Base that Supports the Global Economy,* 1987.

Acid Deposition in the Northeast: 1955

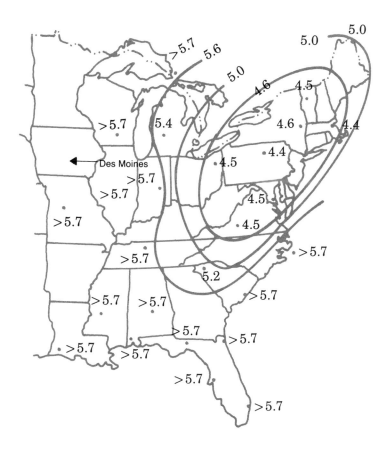

EXPLANATION
- 5.4   pH at sample site
−4.6− Line of equal pH value

Note: Generally, precipitation relatively unaffected by industrial emissions ranges from a minimum pH of 5.0 to a more common pH of 5.6. A decrease of one pH unit (from 5.4 to 4.4 for example) is equivalent to a tenfold increase in acidity.

Source: Likens and Butler, 1981, as cited by the U.S. Geological Survey, *An Evaluation of Trends in the Acidity of Precipitation and the Related Acidification of Surface Water in North America,* Water-Supply Paper 2249, Figure 3, 1983.

Acid Deposition in the United States: 1984

Source: Pacific Northwest Laboratory, *Acid Precipitation in North America:*
1984 Annual and Seasonal Summaries from the ADS Data Base, 1987 as cited
by World Resources Institute and International Institute for Environment and
Development, *World Resources 1987; An Assessment of the Resource Base that*
Supports the Global Economy, Figure 25.3, 1987.

pH Scale

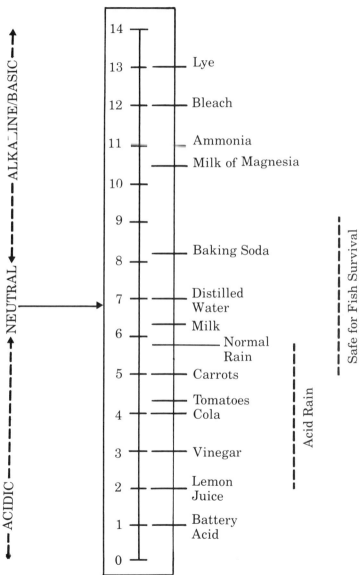

Acidified and Threatened Lakes by State: 1986
(States listed by region)

Acid neutralizing capacity measures (in microequivalents, or µeq) the ability of a variety of trace components in water to change incoming acids to neutral compounds. Lakes that have limestone surrounding them, for example, are naturally buffered as lime washes into the lakes. Lakes with an acid neutralizing capacity (ANC) of < = 0 are already acidified and essentially dead. Those with an ANC of < = 50 are close to acidification. And those with an ANC of < = 200 are significantly endangered by acidification.

State	Total Lakes	Number Sampled	Acid Neutralizing Capacity (µeq per liter) (Estimates based on sample) < = 0	< = 50	< = 200	Percent of Lakes Threatened or Acidified
Maine	1966	225	8	200	1337	78.6
Vermont	258	29	0	19	90	34.9
New Hampshire	639	69	17	171	537	84.0
Massachusetts	926	97	52	239	578	62.4
Rhode Island	113	15	13	33	86	76.1
Connecticut	346	24	47	47	145	41.9
New York	2041	191	168	577	1200	58.8
Pennsylvania	616	106	20	79	284	46.1
North Carolina	55	30	0	4	35	63.6
South Carolina	40	12	0	0	10	25.0
Georgia	155	54	10	10	49	31.6
Florida	2088	138	453	732	1146	54.9
Michigan	2073	160	107	368	704	34.0
Wisconsin	3402	253	41	801	1690	49.7
Minnesota	3026	174	0	143	1124	37.1
Washington	1338	117	0	219	822	61.4
Oregon	551	55	0	113	461	83.7
California	2390	147	0	880	2078	86.9
Idaho	972	72	0	189	599	61.6
Montana	1597	80	0	160	824	51.6
Wyoming	1480	83	0	94	1068	72.2
Utah	548	30	0	20	484	88.3
Colorado	1476	132	0	70	591	40.0

Note: In New England, all lakes were tested. Elsewhere, the Environmental Protection Agency chose the most endangered areas for study. States listed include only those with more than 10 lakes sampled. All samples of less than 20 lakes have very large margins of error.

Source: U.S. Environmental Protection Agency, *Characteristics of Lakes in the Eastern United States,* EPA/600/4-86/007a, Table 4-12, 1986; *Characteristics of Lakes in the Western United States,* EPA/600/3-86/054a, Table 5-10, 1986.

Chapter 12

Not in My Backyard: Municipal and Hazardous Wastes

A Growing Mountain of Trash
Hazardous Wastes: Production and Disposal
Living with Toxics
Groundwater Protection at Hazardous Waste Sites

Not in My Backyard:
Municipal and Hazardous Wastes

America is hooked on convenience, packaging and disposables, earning us dubious distinction as the world's top garbage-producing country. In addition, the nation's energy production, plus industry and transportation systems generate toxic substances which poison our land and water and jeopardize our public health.

A Growing Mountain of Trash

The average American produced almost three-and-a-half pounds of garbage, trash and other throwaways every day in 1984, up 37% from 1960. Nearly 40% of this discarded waste was paper and paperboard. The combined 1984 national total was almost 150 million tons of waste, only 15 million tons of which was recycled (page 143).

Many states have run out of landfill space and ship their refuse out of state, although fewer and fewer of their neighbors are willing to accept it. The now-famous odyssey of the Islip, N.Y. garbage barge whose load was rejected by six states and three countries graphically illustrates the nation's growing waste-disposal crisis.

Hazardous Wastes: Production and Disposal

In addition to municipal wastes, we generated 264 million metric tons of hazardous wastes in 1981. New Jersey produced almost 40% of the total, followed by Texas, with 22%, and Louisiana, with 11% (page 144).

Most of the nation's 27,000 identified hazardous waste disposal sites contain heavy metals and/or chemicals which are known to cause neurological disorders, hypertension, heart disease and cancer in humans. Toxic substances dumped in landfills, surface impoundments and drums leach into the soil, escape into the air, poison drinking water and sometimes force temporary evacuations or even permanent relocation of area residents.

The Environmental Protection Agency has included or proposed inclusion of fewer than 800 hazardous waste sites on its National Priorities List (NPL), making them eligible for cleanup using federal Superfund money (page 146). EPA noted in 1986 that hazardous materials had leached into groundwater at almost three quarters of Superfund sites, that contaminated surface water was found at about 44% of the sites and that airborne toxics had been detected at 15% of the sites.

Living with Toxics

According to the Council on Economic Priorities, 8 of 10 Americans live near one of the nation's more than 22,000 identified toxic waste sites.

New Jersey leads the nation in the number of Superfund sites within its borders (96), followed by New York, Pennsylvania, Michigan and California (page 148). Alaska, Hawaii and Nevada are the only states without a Superfund site.

The Centers for Disease Control reports that in 1980 nearly half of U.S. residents lived in counties which contained a Superfund site (page 149). Almost 54% of those who lived in counties located in metropolitan areas were affected, while about a quarter of those who lived in non-metropolitan area counties were affected. In the Northeast and West, about 65% of the population lived in a county with a Superfund site, while in the South and Midwest, about a third of the population lived in a county with such a site.

Groundwater Protection at Hazardous Waste Sites

Well systems designed to protect groundwater at hazardous waste sites are generally inadequate (page 150). Only 41% of the more than 1,200 hazardous waste disposal facilities subject to groundwater monitoring had even nominally adequate well systems in 1984, while 25% of the facilities had inadequate well systems and 15% had no wells at all. No wells in Arizona, Hawaii, Idaho, Maine, Montana, New Hampshire and Nevada were adequately protected, while large numbers of hazardous waste sites in California, Connecticut and Texas either had no wells, inadequate wells or wells listed as "status unknown."

Municipal Solid Waste Generation and Recovery: 1960 to 1984

(Millions of tons, except where indicated)

Item and Material	1960	1965	1970	1975	1980	1984
Gross waste generated	82.3	98.3	118.3	122.7	139.1	148.1
Per person per day in pounds	2.50	2.77	3.16	3.11	3.35	3.43
Resources recovered	5.9	6.2	8.0	9.1	13.4	15.1
Per person per day in pounds	.18	.17	.21	.23	.32	.35

Note: Data covers residential and commercial solid wastes which comprise the major portion of typical municipal collections. Excludes mining, agricultural and industrial processing, demolition and construction wastes, sewage sludge, and junked autos and obsolete equipment wastes.

Source: Franklin Associates, Ltd. (for the U.S. Environmental Protection Agency), *Characterization of Municipal Solid Waste in the United States, 1960 to 2000*, 1986, as cited by the U.S. Bureau of the Census, *Statistical Abstract of the United States, 1987*, Table 335, 1987.

Quantity of Hazardous Waste
Generated by State: 1981

State	Amount Produced (Metric tons)	Percent of National Total
United States	263,939,241	100.0
Alabama	2,117,857	0.8
Alaska	26	0.0
Arizona	109,859	0.0
Arkansas	430,626	0.2
California	6,026,775	2.3
Colorado	32,715	0.0
Connecticut	2,056,044	0.8
Delaware	12,866	0.0
Florida	5,188,225	2.0
Georgia	227,341	0.1
Hawaii	64,477	0.0
Idaho	4,458	0.0
Illinois	482,323	0.2
Indiana	4,160,851	1.6
Iowa	54,947	0.0
Kansas	268,454	0.1
Kentucky	9,382,520	3.6
Louisiana	30,289,926	11.5
Maine	4,278	0.0
Maryland	156,894	0.1
Massachusetts	385,242	0.1
Michigan	4,536,860	1.7
Minnesota	24,758	0.0
Mississippi	1,545,537	0.6
Missouri	108,915	0.0
Montana	207	0.0
Nebraska	8,403	0.0

Continued, next page

Quantity of Hazardous Waste
Generated by State: 1981 (Cont.)

State	Amount Produced (Metric tons)	Percent of National Total
United States	**263,939,241**	**100.0**
Nevada	943,587	0.4
New Hampshire	71,391	0.0
New Jersey	104,748,815	39.7
New Mexico	106,653	0.0
New York	1,304,390	0.5
North Carolina	944,799	0.4
North Dakota	25	0.0
Ohio	8,059,196	3.1
Oklahoma	1,919,514	0.7
Oregon	57,646	0.0
Pennsylvania	3,402,216	1.3
Rhode Island	23,192	0.0
South Carolina	646,586	0.2
South Dakota	26	0.0
Tennessee	539,156	0.2
Texas	58,933,850	22.3
Utah	128,539	0.0
Vermont	1,468	0.0
Virginia	16,331	0.0
Washington	65,322	0.0
West Virginia	13,828,907	5.2
Wisconsin	77,855	0.0
Wyoming	56,670	0.0

Note: Amount of waste produced per state is estimated from samples taken within each state.

Source: U.S. Environmental Protection Agency and Development Planning and Research Associates, Inc., unpublished data 1981 RIA Mail Survey, 1987.

Number of Superfund Sites by State: 1987

Superfund is a federally administered program which finances the cleanup of waste spills and abandoned waste disposal sites.

State	Number of Sites*	Rank
United States	**793**	–
Alabama	9	22**
Alaska	0	48**
Arizona	6	32**
Arkansas	9	22**
California	48	5
Colorado	13	16**
Connecticut	7	28**
Delaware	12	18**
Florida	34	7
Georgia	4	39**
Hawaii	0	48**
Idaho	4	39**
Illinois	17	14
Indiana	24	10
Iowa	7	28**
Kansas	7	28**
Kentucky	10	21
Louisiana	6	32**
Maine	6	32**
Maryland	7	28**
Massachusetts	21	13
Michigan	58	4
Minnesota	40	6
Mississippi	2	43**
Missouri	14	15
Montana	8	26**
Nebraska	3	42

Continued, next page

Number of Superfund Sites by State: 1987 (Cont.)

State	Number of Sites*	Rank
United States	**793**	—
Nevada	0	48**
New Hampshire	13	16**
New Jersey	96	1
New Mexico	4	39**
New York	63	2
North Carolina	9	22**
North Dakota	1	45**
Ohio	28	9
Oklahoma	6	32**
Oregon	5	36**
Pennsylvania	61	3
Rhode Island	8	26**
South Carolina	12	18**
South Dakota	1	45**
Tennessee	9	22**
Texas	22	12
Utah	5	36**
Vermont	2	43**
Virginia	11	20
Washington	23	11
West Virginia	5	36**
Wisconsin	32	8
Wyoming	1	45**

*Includes both national and federal sites.
**Tie

Sources: U.S. Environmental Protection Agency, *National Priorities List Fact Book*, June 1986; and U.S. Government Printing Office, *Federal Register*, Part III, July 22, 1987.

Number of Superfund Sites by State: 1987

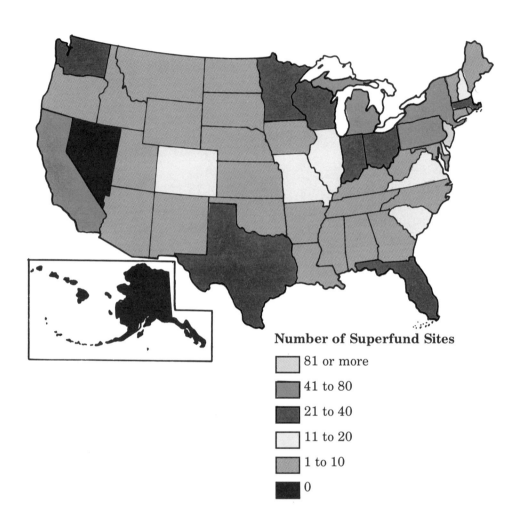

Number of Superfund Sites

	81 or more
	41 to 80
	21 to 40
	11 to 20
	1 to 10
	0

Sources: U.S. Environmental Protection Agency, *National Priorities List Fact Book*, HW-7.3, June 1986; U.S. Government Printing Office, *Federal Register*, Part III, July 22, 1987.

Population in Counties
with Superfund Sites: 1980
(Numbers in hundreds of thousands)

Region*	-------- All Areas --------		
	Total Population	Percent in Affected Counties	Population in Affected Counties
Total	**2,265**	**45.7**	**1,035**
Northeast	491	64.9	319
Midwest	589	37.8	223
South	751	29.0	219
West	432	63.7	275

Region*	-------- Metro Areas --------		
	Total Population	Percent in Affected Counties	Population in Affected Counties
Total	**1,600**	**53.9**	**862**
Northeast	323	63.6	205
Midwest	417	46.8	195
South	504	39.9	201
West	356	73.0	260

Region*	-------- Non-metro Areas --------		
	Total Population	Percent in Affected Counties	Population in Affected Counties
Total	**666**	**26.1**	**174**
Northeast	169	67.4	114
Midwest	172	15.8	27
South	250	7.1	18
West	76	19.7	15

*Regions are defined as follows: Northeast includes ME, NH,VT, MA, RI, CT, NY, NJ and PA; Midwest includes OH, IN, IL, MI, WI, MN, IA, MO, ND, SD, NE and KS; South includes DE, MD, VA, WV, NC, SC, GA, FL, KY, TN, AL, AR, LA, OK, TX and MS; West includes MT, ID, WY, CO, NM, AZ, UT, NV, WA, OR, CA, AK and HI.

Source: John E. Anderson, Ph.D., *U.S. Population Distribution and the Location of Hazardous Waste Sites,* Centers for Disease Control, Table 8, 1986.

Status of Groundwater-Protection Well Systems at Hazardous Waste Sites by State: 1984

State	Facilities Subject to Monitoring	Number Inadequate	Number No Wells	Status Unknown	Inadequate/Unknown TOTAL	PERCENT
Alabama	37	7	7	11	25	68
Alaska	0	0	0	0	0	0
Arizona	7	1	4	2	7	100
Arkansas	18	8	1	4	13	72
California	93	28	13	49	90	97
Colorado	13	3	5	1	9	69
Connecticut	87	21	18	43	82	94
Delaware	3	1	0	1	2	67
Florida	26	10	2	4	16	62
Georgia	33	4	1	3	8	24
Hawaii	4	0	1	3	4	100
Idaho	4	1	0	3	4	100
Illinois	45	17	5	4	26	58
Indiana	41	7	8	3	18	44
Iowa	11	1	6	3	10	91
Kansas	13	3	2	3	8	62
Kentucky	17	2	2	1	5	29
Louisiana	64	22	12	0	34	53
Maine	4	2	1	1	4	100
Maryland	10	5	0	0	5	50
Massachusetts	15	12	0	2	14	93
Michigan	41	9	2	15	26	63
Minnesota	4	0	0	0	0	0
Mississippi	22	1	0	3	4	18
Missouri	24	8	6	5	19	79
Montana	8	0	0	8	8	100
Nebraska	4	0	2	0	2	50
Nevada	5	1	0	4	5	100
New Hampshire	4	3	0	1	4	100

Continued, next page

Status of Groundwater-Protection Well Systems at Hazardous Waste Sites by State: 1984 (Cont.)

State	Facilities Subject to Monitoring	Number Inadequate	Number No Wells	Status Unknown	Inadequate/Unknown TOTAL	Inadequate/Unknown PERCENT
New Jersey	30	3	0	2	5	17
New Mexico	17	7	4	3	14	82
New York	33	23	2	5	30	91
North Carolina	26	4	0	0	4	15
North Dakota	4	0	0	1	1	25
Ohio	52	15	7	6	28	54
Oklahoma	27	5	3	0	8	30
Oregon	8	2	1	4	7	88
Pennsylvania	68	10	8	4	22	32
Rhode Island	0	0	0	0	0	0
South Carolina	32	12	2	3	17	53
South Dakota	0	0	0	0	0	0
Tennessee	14	1	2	3	6	43
Texas	174	22	44	12	78	45
Utah	18	3	4	4	11	61
Vermont	0	0	0	0	0	0
Virginia	23	3	3	0	6	26
Washington	15	7	2	4	13	87
West Virginia	17	9	0	2	11	65
Wisconsin	7	2	1	0	3	43
Wyoming	11	6	2	1	9	82

Note: Hazardous waste facilities subject to groundwater monitoring include land disposal facilities and surface impoundments used to store, treat or dispose of a variety of hazardous wastes.

Sources: Committee on Energy and Commerce, U.S. House of Representatives, 99th Congress, *Groundwater Monitoring Survey,* April 1985; U.S. Environmental Protection Agency, RCRA/Superfund Hotline, June 1987.

Chapter 13

Land, Habitat and Wildlife:
The Pressure's Killing Them

Soil Erosion
Loss of Wetlands
Contamination of Productive Shellfish Waters
Wildlife Habitat and Endangered Species

Land, Habitat and Wildlife: The Pressure's Killing Them

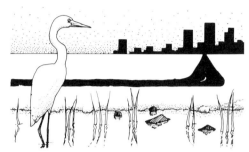

The demands of our growing population endanger the open space, bright water and wildlife that make "America the Beautiful." As we destroy millions of acres of productive land and estuaries through development and push millions of tons of priceless topsoil into our rivers and waterways, we threaten the very survival of numerous plant and animal species.

Soil Erosion

The American Farmland Trust estimates that more than 3 million acres of productive farmland are lost to development each year, or about 320 acres of agricultural land per *hour.* In addition, according to government studies, water erosion strips more than 4 billion tons of topsoil from agricultural land each year, and wind blows another billion tons of soil from improperly protected crop and range land. Erosion of topsoil is 25% greater today than in the Dust Bowl years of the 1930s, and the problem is getting worse.

Much of the increase in soil erosion is blamed on an abandonment of soil-conserving farm practices such as contour plowing, terracing, crop rotation and wind-protective hedge rows, as well as crop production pressures which encourage planting of acreage prone to wind and water damage.

In 1982, the U.S. lost more than 3 billion tons of topsoil to wind and water erosion (page 158). Losses were greatest in the Midwest, where, in Iowa alone, 318 million tons of soil were blown and washed off the land. (The Natural Resources Defense Council reports that some Iowa farms have registered losses of 50 to 60 tons of soil per acre per year.)

Loss of Wetlands

Fresh and salt water wetlands like marshes, swamps and bogs, once regarded as mere obstacles to development, are now recognized for their critical role in flood and erosion control, groundwater recharge and water quality maintenance. In addition, wetlands are among the most productive ecosystems in the world, serving as incubators and nurseries for great numbers of waterfowl and other birds, fish, shellfish and animals. When wetlands are destroyed, the damage is usually irreversible.

Despite their recognized value, hundreds of thousands of acres of the nation's wetlands continue to be eliminated every year by pollution, channelization, dams, dikes, levees, excessive nutrient loading, mining of peat, coal, sand and gravel, draining, dredging, filling, and housing and commercial developments. Of the nearly 215 million original acres of wetlands in the U.S., less than 99 million acres remained by 1970.

According to a trends analysis conducted by the U.S. Fish and Wildlife Service from the mid-1950s to the mid-1970s, certain areas of the country are destroying their wetlands at an alarming annual rate (page 159). Though comprehensive regional and state data are not available, the areas suffering the heaviest observed losses during this 20-year period bordered on the Gulf of Mexico or were clumped in the Mid- and Southern-Atlantic and the upper Midwest.

By 1984, millions of acres of original wetlands had been lost (page 160). Iowa, for example, had depleted its original 2.3 million acres of wetlands to a mere 26,470 acres, while California had eliminated all but 450,000 acres of its original 5 million acres of wetlands.

The Fish and Wildlife Service says it assumes that wetlands losses are continuing at the same rate, although it has not published any new data since its 1984 analysis and does not intend to issue another report until 1990.

Contamination of Productive Shellfish Waters

Birds, mammals, fish, shellfish and their food sources are all vulnerable to human-generated poisons dumped into fresh and marine waters. Bottom-dwelling organisms like shellfish, which spend all of their lives in coastal waters or estuaries, are at particularly serious risk of contamination by bacteria and biotoxins and of death from oxygen depletion.

Rapidly developing regions on the Gulf and South Atlantic coasts have contaminated thousands of acres of shellfish-producing waters with effluent from municipal sewage treatment plants and pleasure boats and runoff from cities, farms and highways.

The 1985 National Shellfish Register report published by the government showed that more than 40% of the productive shellfish areas in the country were restricted to some degree because of water pollution, the failure of officials to adopt shellfish contamination standards and/or proven shellfish contamination (page 161). The vast majority of harvest-limited shellfish waters border the Gulf of Mexico. In states bordering on the Gulf and the Pacific coast, almost 75% of all productive shellfish waters are harvest-limited.

Wildlife Habitat and Endangered Species

Most ecologists agree that reducing the size of a natural habitat increases species' risk of extinction. Timber clear cutting, mining, farming, hunting and the conversion of open space into commercial and residential developments have squeezed many of our native plant and wildlife species into smaller and smaller areas. And, as ZPG founder Dr. Paul R. Ehrlich notes, "Every time we remove a plant species [in the world], we probably eliminate something on the order of 10 animal species."

National parks constitute the last refuge for some wildlife, yet even these protected habitats are simply not large enough to ensure the survival of several species, particularly large native animals (page 162). In Lassen Volcano, California, for example, 43% of the original large animal species can no longer be found in that area.

The U.S. Interior Department's Fish and Wildlife Service and the Department of Commerce's National Marine Fisheries Service are charged with listing endangered and threatened wildlife and enforcing protective regulations and funding species recovery activities. As of March 1987, a total of 376 plant and animal species were listed as endangered or threatened, while a backlog of more than 3,900 candidates for listing awaited action, 315 of which may already be extinct (page 163).

In some states, staggering numbers of plant species are at risk of extinction (page 164). In Hawaii, for example, almost 750 species of plants were considered candidates for the endangered or threatened list in 1985.

Soil Erosion by State and Region: 1982

Region and State	Average Annual Loss (Million tons)	Region and State	Average Annual Loss (Million tons)
United States	**3,087.8**	Virginia	
Northeast	**57.6**	West Virginia	2.8
New England	4.4	North Carolina	45.7
Maine	2.0	South Carolina	12.9
New Hampshire	0.2	Georgia	41.7
Vermont	0.8	Florida	10.5
Massachusetts	0.6	East South Central	199.9
Rhode Island	0.1	Kentucky	56.5
Connecticut	0.7	Tennessee	55.9
Middle Atlantic	53.3	Alabama	32.2
New York	17.4	Mississippi	55.3
New Jersey	4.7	West South Central	658.1
Pennsylvania	31.2	Arkansas	39.7
Midwest	**1,540.3**	Louisiana	29.3
East North Central	410.2	Oklahoma	63.7
Ohio	49.4	Texas	525.4
Indiana	84.7	**West**	**485.3**
Illinois	172.4	Mountain	381.5
Michigan	36.3	Montana	170.0
Wisconsin	67.4	Idaho	50.6
West North Central	1,130.1	Wyoming	4.5
Minnesota	147.8	Colorado	121.6
Iowa	318.0	New Mexico	15.7
Missouri	146.5	Arizona	4.5
North Dakota	136.2	Utah	6.7
South Dakota	89.6	Nevada	8.0
Nebraska	132.1	Pacific	103.8
Kansas	160.0	Washington	53.7
South	**1,004.6**	Oregon	24.7
South Atlantic	146.6	California	23.3
Delaware	2.0	Alaska	n/a
Maryland	9.3	Hawaii	2.1

n/a = not available.

Source: U.S. Bureau of the Census, *State Metropolitan and Data Book, 1986,* Table C. States, 1985.

Recent Wetland Loss Rates:
Mid-1950s to mid-1970s

State or Region	Loss Rate (Acres per Year)
Lower Mississippi Alluvial Plain	165,000
Louisiana's Forested Wetlands	87,200
North Carolina's Pocosins	43,500
Prairie Pothole Region	33,000
Louisiana's Coastal Marshes	25,000
Great Lakes Basin	20,000
Wisconsin	20,000
Michigan	6,500
Kentucky	3,600
New Jersey's Coastal Marshes	3,084*
Palm Beach County, Florida	3,055
Maryland's Coastal Wetlands	1,000*
New York's Estuarine Marshes	740
Delaware's Coastal Marshes	444*

*After passage of state coastal wetland protection laws, New Jersey's loss rate was reduced to 50 acres per year; Maryland's and Delaware's to 20 acres per year.

Source: U.S. Department of the Interior, Fish and Wildlife Service, *Wetlands of the United States: Current Status and Recent Trends,* National Wetlands Inventory, March 1984.

Wetland Losses in Various States:
Late 1700s to 1984

State or Region	Original Wetlands (Acres)	1984 Wetlands (Acres)	Percent of Wetlands Lost
Iowa's Natural Marshes	2,333,000	26,470	99
California	5,000,000	450,000	91
Nebraska's Rainwater Basin	94,000	8,460	91
Mississippi Alluvial Plain	24,000,000	5,200,000	78
Michigan	11,200,000	3,200,000	71
North Dakota	5,000,000	2,000,000	60
Minnesota	18,400,000	8,700,000	53
Louisiana's Forested Wetlands	11,300,000	5,635,000	50
Connecticut's Coastal Marshes	30,000	15,000	50
North Carolina's Pocosins	2,500,000	1,503,000*	40
South Dakota	2,000,000	1,300,000	35
Wisconsin	10,000,000	6,750,000	32

*Only 695,000 acres of Pocosins remain undisturbed; the rest are partially drained, developed or planned for development.

Source: U.S. Department of the Interior, Fish and Wildlife Service, *Wetlands of the United States: Current Status and Recent Trends*, National Wetlands Inventory, March 1984.

Condition of Productive Shellfish Waters: 1985

(Thousands of acres)

Productive waters are those areas which did or could produce shellfish (either naturally or aquaculturally) in quantities sufficient to justify commercial harvesting.

Region and State	Approved for Harvest*	Harvest Limited**	Percent Limited
United States	**9,529**	**6,970**	**42**
Northern Atlantic	**5,537**	**924**	**14**
Maine	936	110	11
New Hampshire	4	6	60
Massachusetts	255	47	16
Rhode Island	96	32	25
Connecticut	309	84	21
New York	828	193	19
New Jersey	236	159	40
Delaware	209	22	10
Maryland	1,369	64	4
Virginia	1,295	207	14
Southern Atlantic	**2,056**	**668**	**25**
North Carolina	1,755	370	17
South Carolina	200	81	29
Georgia	61	144	70
Florida	40	73	65
Gulf of Mexico	**1,773**	**4,982**	**74**
Florida	266	566	68
Alabama	74	298	80
Mississippi	123	267	68
Louisiana	0	3,493	100
Texas	1,310	358	21
West Coast	**163**	**396**	**71**
California	2	276	99
Oregon	14	26	65
Washington	147	94	39

*Approved for harvest are those areas surveyed and found free of hazardous concentrations of harmful organisms and/or pollution.

**Harvest limited includes 1) conditionally approved areas: those approved for only part of the year due to pollution or failure of authorities to establish approved standards during that period, 2) restricted areas: those where shellfish is contaminated, and 3) prohibited areas: those which are closed due to hazardous levels of contamination or areas that have not been surveyed at all.

Source: National Oceanic and Atmospheric Administration and the Department of Health and Human Service, *1985 National Shellfish Register of Classified Estuarine Waters,* 1985, as cited by Office of Technology Assessment, *Wastes in Marine Environments,* Office of Technology Assessment, Table 7, 1987.

Habitat Area and Loss of Large Animal Species in Western National Parks: 1986

Park	Area (Square Miles)	Percent of Original Species Lost
Bryce Canyon, UT	89	36
Lassen Volcano, CA	265	43
Zion, UT	365	36
Crater Lake, OR	398	31
Mount Rainier, WA	606	32
Rocky Mountain, CO	651	31
Yosemite, CA	1,294	25
Sequoia-Kings Canyon, CA	2,105	23
Glacier-Waterton, MT	2,873	7
Grand Teton-Yellowstone, ID-MT-WY	6,414	4

Source: William D. Newmark, "A Land-Bridge Island Perspective on Mammalian Extinctions in Western North America Parks," *Nature,* January 29, 1987, as cited by Edward C. Wolf in "On the Brink of Extinction: Conserving the Diversity of Life," Worldwatch Paper 78, Worldwatch Institute, Table 3, June 1987.

Threatened and Endangered Species and Candidates for Listing: March 1987

Category 1 includes plants and animals whose biological vulnerability to extinction is well-documented and which warrant official proposal as endangered or threatened species.

Category 2 includes plants and animals which may merit protection as endangered or threatened species, but further documentation of their biological vulnerability to threat is needed to justify official proposal.

| Category | Number of Species Listed as Endangered or Threatened | ---- Number of Candidates for Listing ---- | | | |
		Category 1: Completed Research	Category 2: Need More Research	Total Candidates	Possibly Already Extinct
Total Candidates	**376**	**962**	**2951**	**3913**	**315**
Plants	145	894	1623	2517	204
Vertebrates	182	35	480	515	20
Invertebrates	49	33	848	881	91

Notes: Species include only those which live in the U.S. and its territories and does not include those that annually migrate to foreign countries. The candidate lists are continuously revised as new information becomes available. Official revised lists are published every few years. Apparent trends do not necessarily infer changes in circumstances. Candidate species have no legal standing simply by virtue of being candidates for listing.

Sources: U.S. Department of the Interior, Fish and Wildlife Service, *Endangered Species Technical Bulletin,* Vol. XII, No. 4, April 1987; Defenders of Wildlife, *Saving Endangered Species, Amending and Implementing the Endangered Species Act,* Table 2, July 1986; and U.S. Department of the Interior, Fish and Wildlife Service, unpublished data, 1987.

Candidates for Endangered and Threatened Plant Species List in Five Leading States: 1985

State	Total Candidates	Category 1*: Completed Research	Category 2*: Need More Research
Hawaii	748	551	197
California	655	121	534
Florida	177	38	139
Oregon	131	8	123
Texas	125	13	112

*See preceding page for definition of categories.

Source: U.S. Department of Interior, Fish and Wildlife Service, 1986, as cited by Defenders of Wildlife, *Saving Endangered Species, Amending and Implementing the Endangered Species Act*, Defenders of Wildlife, Table 3, July 1986.